Your Kid's *a* BRAT *and* It's All Your Fault

Elaine Rose Glickman

A TarcherPerigee Book

An imprint of Penguin Random House LLC
375 Hudson Street
New York, New York 10014

Most TarcherPerigee books are available at special quantity discounts for bulk purchase for sales promotions, premiums, fund-raising, and educational needs. Special books or book excerpts also can be created to fit specific needs. For details, write: SpecialMarkets@penguinrandomhouse.com.

Library of Congress Cataloging-in-Publication Data

Names: Glickman, Elaine Rose, author.
Title: Your kid's a brat and it's all your fault : nip the attitude in the bud—from toddler to tween / Elaine Rose Glickman.
Description: New York : Tarcher, 2016.
Identifiers: LCCN 2015045423 | ISBN 9780399173127 (paperback)
Subjects: LCSH: Parenting. | Parent and child. | Pampered child syndrome. | Problem children—Behavior modification. | BISAC: FAMILY & RELATIONSHIPS /
Parenting / General. | FAMILY & RELATIONSHIPS / Life Stages / School Age.
Classification: LCC HQ755.8 .G584 2016 | DDC 649/.1—dc23

Printed in the United States of America
1 3 5 7 9 10 8 6 4 2

Some names and identifying characteristics have been changed to protect the privacy of the individuals involved.

CONTENTS

INTRODUCTION: YOUR KID'S A BRAT

◆ ◆ ◆ ◆ ◆ ◆ ◆ ◆

We've heard them—kids ordering their parents to shut up. We've seen them—kids pushing past grown-ups into the elevator. We've met them—kids who whine and bite and never say thank you and have better phones than we do.

Maybe some of these kids are even our own.

We know their other sides, of course. These kids are also smart and sweet and funny and capable and affectionate. They get stressed out at school; they're influenced by the media and advertisements and (less worthy) friends; they've endured countless phases and growth spurts and challenges. They're living in a culture that glorifies violence, sexualizes children, and encourages kids not to be kind or responsible or mature but to be cool—to mouth off to grown-ups and acquire expensive stuff and look hot and generally act like sort of a jerk.

We know our smallest kids are affected, too. They learn bad manners when they hear adults speaking rudely to one another.

They learn that appearances matter when beaming strangers proclaim them beautiful. They learn to prefer unhealthy meals when they see PBS Kids shilling for Chuck E. Cheese's.

We know that society is doing an excellent job turning our wonderful children into inconsiderate, demanding, materialistic, self-centered, disrespectful, junk-food-craving brats.

The problem is that sometimes we do the same.

Our intentions are good. We want our kids to be happy, so we hesitate to tell them no. We want our kids to express their opinions, so we let them talk back. We want our kids to be well fed and well rested, so we overlook misbehaviors during dinner and at bedtime. We want our kids to feel important, so we let them call the shots.

But one day we turn around and realize that we've got on our hands indulged, disagreeable children who are rarely told no and eat only five foods. And as wonderful as these children may nevertheless appear to us, we must admit that in many parts of the universe they would be called brats.

And that is the ultimate irony. In our quest to give our children the best—to provide every comfort, every advantage, every peak experience, every drop of self-esteem—we are actually failing them pretty badly.

No one likes a brat. Not teachers, not coaches, not babysitters, not other parents. And certainly not the adults who will someday be interviewing our children for admission to a prestigious college or evaluating their prospective value as an employee or considering becoming their spouse.

If we truly want our kids to be happy and cherished and successful, we have to teach them, well, not to be a brat. For our sake and the sake of those around us, yes. But also for their own.

Because it's not only those around our kids who would strongly prefer they not be brats. It's also our kids themselves.

A toddler shrieking in the checkout line may appear to want a Push Pop. A third grader rolling his eyes may appear to want a more accommodating parent. A tween demanding to wear a skirt so short you can see her thong underwear may appear to want popularity and male attention. But what they really want are limits and boundaries and consistent expectations. What they want are opportunities to learn discipline, to demonstrate responsibility, to develop self-esteem, to earn self-respect and the respect of those around them. What they want, deep down, is for us—their parents—to step up. To say, no, stop it, that's not okay. To say, you don't need to act like a brat to get my attention or to get what you want. To say, I love you enough to teach you a better way.

In the short term, the brat with the cowed parents may seem to have it pretty good. But in the long term, that's not who we want our kids to be. In the long term, that's not who they want to be, either.

So how do we stop our kids from becoming—or continuing to act like—brats? This book will help us learn how to recognize situations in which we are enabling—or even encouraging—bratty behavior; how to see our children, and our parenting, as others do; how to change unhealthy patterns and make things better—for our kids, for those around them, for our families, for ourselves; and how to step up and be the parents our kids deserve.

Even if those kids are, at the moment, stretched out on the couch, feet propped on the coffee table, hollering for a soda. Go ahead and pour them a drink (don't forget the crushed ice!)—but you might want to warn them it's last call. Things are about to change.

SECTION 1

Your Budding **BRAT**—Toddlers and Preschoolers

INTRODUCING YOUR BUDDING BRAT

◆ ◆ ◆ ◆ ◆ ◆ ◆ ◆

Of course your kid is the most precious creature in the universe, and of course you love her with every ounce of your being, and of course you revel in every amazing thing she does, especially those amazing things her peers are not yet doing, probably because they eat so many processed foods. But . . .

But have you noticed that your kid is developing a couple of habits that are a tad less than delightful? Maybe telling you what to do, like, a lot; maybe kicking you if you dare to disobey; maybe emitting loud and unrelenting shrieks at bedtime or in the checkout line or at a restaurant (or all of the above, hooray!). And not that you have any ambivalence about your kid's wonderfulness, because she is totally special and extraordinary—but if you were to be one hundred percent honest, you might admit that, well, these habits are a teeny bit annoying. And that you and she might be a lot happier if she would cut it out.

I have two awesome pieces of news for you: One, you are

absolutely right. And two, feeling this way does not make you a bad parent.

I realize you may have heard differently. I am aware that being a good parent has come to mean letting your kid do whatever she wants, and smiling beatifically as she runs amok. I am aware that your kid's biting and hitting have been rebranded as avenues of self-expression. I am aware that telling your kid to stop finger painting the cat has become equated with crushing her creative potential forever and ever. I am even aware of the terrible consequences said to lie in store for the kid whose parent dares to tell her no: shredded self-esteem, a stunted capacity for attachment, self-destructive attempts to cope with existential angst that ultimately result in a stint on *Teen Mom* or—best-case scenario—the wait list at her first-choice college.

What I do not understand is why you believe this shit. Do you honestly think that beaming as your kid yells at you, forcing a laugh as she smacks you in front of your friends, earnestly asking about her "mad feelings" as she hurls her dinner plate at the wall, and letting her supplant your spouse in the marital bed is setting your kid on the path to a happy, healthy life? Are you sincerely convinced that your kid—the one who's been screaming for ten straight ear-splitting minutes—is so fragile that her entire future will be unhinged because you turned off *Frozen* and made her go to bed? And do you really want to live in a home where your role is not to parent and guide and teach your kid—but to attend slavishly to her every whim and desire?

If the answer to even one of these questions is no, this section is for you. In the following chapters, I'll examine the not-so-charming behaviors emerging in your budding brat, exploring why your kid is acting this way, what her whining/clinging/refusing to sleep, etc., really mean, and how to respond calmly, lovingly—and extremely effectively. You'll find plenty of pep talks to remind you who the actual boss should be in the relationship between parent and kid (hint: It's not the one wearing size three *Frozen* underpants, unless you are a seriously kinky person), easy and practical guidance for redirecting your kid when she's going completely off the rails, and insight on helping your kid deal with the chaotic and tumultuous emotions she's experiencing as a toddler and preschooler. (These years aren't exactly easy for her, either!) And while I make no guarantees—results may vary, and all that shit—this section will truly benefit your kid every bit as much as it benefits you, and your budding brat will be thrilled and relieved to realize that you love her enough to step up and teach her a better way. I almost promise.

YOUR KID BOSSES YOU AROUND

◆ ◆ ◆ ◆ ◆ ◆ ◆

Here is a list of prestigious jobs held by people I have encountered in the last several years:

Surgeon

Attorney (like, a really well-compensated partner, not a just-out-of-law-school-and-miserably-paying-dues associate)

Entrepreneur

CEO

Independently wealthy person (I have no idea where the money came from, but there is a lot of it)

Computer genius

All the people holding these jobs have this in common: Their young kids boss them around like you would not believe.

Then again, maybe you would. Because if you're reading this chapter, it's a good bet that your kid is doing the same to you.

Do you remember being little and having your parents do everything you wanted? Remember the rush you got when you didn't have to say a word—you just pointed and grunted at something, and your parents jumped up to bring it to you? Remember when they wouldn't let you have your way, so you scrunched up your face and went "unnnnnh" until they gave in? Remember that time they told you no, and you had to make a couple of angry noises to put them in their place and make sure they didn't try that shit again?

Yeah, I don't remember any of that, either. But I bet your kid does.

It's like you have a secret life or something. Think of how you behave with other adults: If some jerk tries to cut you off in traffic, you don't automatically cede your spot, then roll down your window to apologize for being in his way and toss him fifty bucks for his troubles. If a colleague at work tells you to finish the project on your own while she takes a nap under her desk, you don't beam and respond that that sounds great, and you'll take her calls, too, so the phone won't disturb her. You may let your supervisor at the office or the alpha mom at your kid's preschool put you down a little bit, but in general you conduct yourself with a certain amount of confidence, poise, and dignity, right?

But that all flies out the window the second your kid tells you to do something. No matter how many degrees you have, no matter how many employees you oversee, no matter how many people hang on your every word about fashion or vaccines or stocks or asteroids or climate change or crowdsourcing, you turn into a blithering idiot (no offense), ready to hear and heed whatever ridiculous order emerges from your kid's mouth. So you may be perfectly comfortable in a chair, but you leap out of it because your kid's demanding to sit there. You may not actually want your kid playing with your engagement ring, but you hand it over because, you know, she's tugging at it. You may not like your kid's order to "go over there" and "leave me alone," especially when doing so will leave her alone with a box of cookies, but you obey because, well, you just do.

I understand what you're trying to do, and even though I may not sound like it, I'm actually pretty sympathetic. You know how hard it is to be a toddler (though maybe it's not so hard to be yours), and you want your kid to feel heard, valued, and loved. You don't get to spend as many hours with your kid as you'd like, and you want the time you do have together to be positive and fun for her. You hate seeing your kid act sad or upset, and she acts sad and upset when you don't do what she says. You want your kid to know she can count on you, and letting her boss you around seems to prove that you're on her side and in her corner.

The problem is that letting your kid boss you around doesn't really help with any of this. While she may appear to be having an awesome time running the show, and while she may look completely comfortable in her role as Boss of You and Your Home, she's got a secret life just like you do. Except in your kid's secret life, she's freaking out. Rather than thriving under your reliability, care, and protection, your kid is growing more terrified with every exchange.

Rather than learning that she can depend on you, your kid is wondering if anyone is ever going to step up and take control.

This is how the current dynamic feels to your kid:

Imagine that you're sick and don't know exactly what's wrong, so you go to a doctor. You're feeling pretty bad, plus you're nervous about all the superbugs being created by overuse of antibiotics, and as soon as the doctor enters the treatment room, you hear yourself blurt out rudely, "Just so you know, I really don't like taking antibiotics." Instead of nodding briefly, examining you, and telling you what the problem is and how to get rid of it, the doctor backs away anxiously. "Okay," she says, "no antibiotics. Got it. Here, um"—she fumbles with her prescription pad and scribbles something—"here's the name of a homeopathic remedy that might help." "Wait," you call as she retreats, "aren't you going to check me out?" But the doctor's too intimidated by you to respond.

Or if you're not so into conventional medicine (but please get your kids vaccinated anyway, I mean, really), imagine that you're getting on an airplane, and when the pilot overhears you telling the flight attendant that the cabin looks filthy, he cancels the trip. Or that you meet the president of the United States and tell her that you think war is immoral, and she immediately disbands the armed forces.

It's fun having this power for about thirty seconds, right? But pretty soon you're feeling awful—bewildered by these experts who let your posturing derail them from carrying out their responsibilities, angry at the people who are supposed to be in charge for failing to maintain control, and wondering how you can give up the reins of authority and put things back the way they're supposed to be.

Because you were just looking for a little attention, just trying to push the envelope, just trying to assert yourself—you didn't actually want to be the boss.

Under all her pointing and grunting and ordering you around, this is how your kid really feels. Sure, it was fun at first—fun to exercise some power, fun to keep the grown-ups on the run, fun to have her bidding done. But now it's pretty awful. Because just like you count on doctors and pilots and presidents to know what the fuck is going on and to keep you safe, your kid is counting on you. Just like you feel better knowing that someone trained and knowledgeable and trustworthy is in charge of things outside your area of expertise, your kid feels better knowing you're the boss.

Realizing this will give you an extra boost of confidence in changing the dynamic between you and your kid—but even if you're not one hundred percent sure I'm right about this one (I am), the dynamic needs to change anyway. A competent adult being bossed around by an otherwise-adorable kid is not nearly as cute as you might think (a giggly, half-apologetic "She loves to be in charge!" charms no one, I am sorry to say), and the situation only gets worse. Your kid will not miraculously outgrow bossing you around, nor will it get easier when she's old enough to "use her words"—she'll only use them to further her cause, and you will find yourself engaged in complicated negotiations over everything from bedtime to homework to why you will absolutely not take her to Riley's party when she has not cleaned her room in weeks except that of course you will. And those twinges of regret and annoyance you now feel as you kowtow to your kid's commands to "get me playdough" and "unhhh!—the *blue* playdough!" will magnify over time—and before you know it, you will wake up to find that your precious angel has morphed into an arrogant, demanding tween and you will read the last chapter of this book and think remorsefully of how much more pleasant the intervening years would have been if you had taken this section to heart.

It's easy for me to tell you to change the dynamic, right? Well, luckily, it's easy for you to do, too. Even if you're still not one hundred percent sure I'm right about this one (I still am), at least dare to imagine that you're old enough and competent enough to be the boss of your own kid rather than the other way around. With this attitude in place, you can listen to, evaluate, and respond appropriately to your kid's requests rather than automatically hopping to: "I hear you want to sit in the chair, but I'm sitting here. You can sit on my lap or on the couch." "I hear you want to play with my ring, but the ring stays on my finger. You can look at it or play with something else." "I hear you want me to leave you alone, but you need a grown-up with you in the kitchen. We can stay here, or you can go into your room by yourself." "I hear you don't want to get into your crib, but it's time for your nap. You can go to sleep, or you can lie here and scream." (I actually used this one when my daughter was a toddler; she looked at me with narrowed eyes and responded, "I. Will. Scream." Which she did. For an hour. Years later, though, it's one of our favorite memories.) These answers may feel stilted, but soon enough they'll be flowing from your lips. They accomplish what you were hoping to accomplish by letting your kid boss you around—they assure your kid that she's been heard and that her wishes are important to you—but they also remind your kid who's in charge. By providing your kid with a choice (sitting on your lap or sitting on the couch, looking at your ring or finding another toy), statements like these allow your kid a sense of control—but keep her from running the entire show. And by providing a template for reacting to your kid's demands, these responses help you stay calm and firm in the face of her attempts to boss you around. Or of her screaming, as the case may be.

Will this new dynamic be an instant hit with your kid? Of course not! She'll resent the shit out of it, at least at first; but if you remain serene and consistent, it won't be long before she adjusts quite nicely to the new reality. And in the meantime, don't worry that she's resenting it; you and your kid might as well learn now that a major part of your job is to do things that are in her best interest but will piss her off mightily. And while she seems bigger than the universe to you, she's actually still very small and pretty much without resources for punishing you for foiling her fantasy of world domination. She can't dock your pay, seize your 401(k), or even take away the car keys, as long as you put them up on a counter she can't reach. Sure, she can whine and grunt and fuss—but once you've read this book, even those ploys will have zero effect.

I mean it, zero. Seriously, quit rolling your eyes and just keep reading.

YOUR KID WHINES

◆ ◆ ◆ ◆ ◆ ◆ ◆ ◆

A couple of years ago, I was teaching some three-year-olds about caring for the environment. Don't laugh; it actually went pretty well. Here's a sample exchange:

> ME: So there are lots of things we can do to help the trees grow, right? Savannah, what's your favorite idea that we've talked about so far?
>
> SAVANNAH (pausing to remove her fingers from her mouth): I like strawberries.
>
> ME: Yes, I like strawberries, too! [I don't.] And if we give our strawberry plants water and sunlight, they'll grow strong and healthy. Declan, what would you give your plant to help it grow?
>
> DECLAN (alarmingly): I drew a gun. See? I would give it a gun.

After further probing, Declan clarified that the gun in question was not what he called a "bullety gun" but simply a water gun, a revelation that provided immense relief and is also completely beside the point I am trying to make. Which is this: Teaching these kids about nature was totally fun. Yes, they went way off topic. Yes, they said all kinds of crazy shit. But they said it earnestly and sweetly. Simply put, they didn't whine.

Have you considered how much more adorable kids are when they don't whine? I wonder if this thought crosses their minds as well, if they hear themselves go, "Noooooooo-uuh, I want that one!" and think, Wow, I really sound like an asshole, maybe I should cut it out—then realize, Nah. Sure, I sound like a jerk, but whining's so damn *effective.*

Yes, effective. Obviously, whining is irritating, annoying, and insanity inducing—but those aspects of whining fail to account for the tremendous amount of time your kid spends engaged in it. After all, if your kid's goal were merely to irritate/annoy/induce insanity, he would find many more enjoyable methods at his disposal—hiding the remote control and forgetting where he put it, perhaps, or peeing in the ball pit you inexplicably bought him and which now dominates your living room. (Wait, that was me.) But that's not why he's whining.

Your kid is whining because whining is one of the most potent tools he has in his arsenal. He's whining because he feels things strongly, and he likes to express those feelings loudly, repeatedly, and determinedly to whoever appears to be in charge of the situation, especially if that person happens to be you. And—most of all—he's whining because he wants something, and because you've taught him that whining is the way to get it.

Quit glancing around to see who I'm looking at—I am totally looking at you. At least, I'm looking at you if you have ever done any of the following:

Told your kid to stop whining and taken absolutely no action when he continued to whine

Told your kid, "I'm not going to listen to you whine," while continuing to listen to him whine

Told your kid no, then relented after he started whining

Told your kid no, held fast to that no when he started whining, then relented after ten minutes of further whining

Used the phrase, "Fine! Here's the cookie. Now please stop whining," with your kid

So yeah, whining is working out quite well for your kid. And he's certainly not going to change the behavior just because it's rude or bothersome or bratty. In fact, there's really just one way to change your kid's whiny behavior: Change your own.

Here's your current game plan: You can't stand hearing your kid whine, so you tell him to stop—but he doesn't. So now what? You would really like him to stop following you around the house, bleating about watching *Planes: Fire & Rescue* and eating fruit snacks and shit, so you give in to his demands. Immediately your kid returns to happy-loving-huggy mode, peace and contentment descend upon the house, and all is well.

All is well, that is, until the next time your kid wants something. Because you've just taught your kid that whining works.

Rather than reacting to your kid's whining in the moment, and making your immediate and only goal ending the whine, please accept this unfortunate but important truth: You cannot force your kid to stop whining. All you can do is guide your kid to realize that whining is ineffective. As soon as this realization sinks in—boom!—the whining stops.

Sounds magical, doesn't it? And it's not even that hard! The hardest part is the first step—but, once taken, it's a step that will set you squarely on the path to liberation not just from whining but from bratdom in general. This first step is immunizing yourself against your kid's whining.

Imagine yourself on an airplane. Your kid is stashed with your in-laws for a couple of days so you and your spouse can enjoy a romantic getaway, maybe, or a relative is handling kid care while you embark on a weekend with the girls. You're settled happily in the first-class cabin (remember, I said "imagine"—if this is actually your life, I'm profoundly jealous, and you should be the one writing a book) and sipping your preflight beverage when, five rows behind you, a kid starts loudly whining. How do you feel?

You feel mildly interested but mostly annoyed, right? How don't you feel? You don't feel anxious or overwhelmed. You don't feel responsible for the kid's distress, or certain that his whining indicates he has a bad or uncaring parent. You feel that sometimes kids whine, and it's irritating. And then you try to ignore it and get back to your life.

Okay, now I want you to imagine that that whining kid is your own and to react in the same way—with a certain level of concern, sure, but without the accompanying flood of my-kid-is-unhappy-and-it's-my-fault-and-I-have-to-make-it-better guilt or the this-whining-makes-me-crazy-but-I-need-to-interact-with-my-child-smilingly-and-positively-at-all-times panic. Because you were right the first time: A kid's whining doesn't mean he has a Neglectful Parent or that he's being failed in some horrible way or that he requires patient attendance to his moaning and groaning. It really doesn't. And as soon as you accept that fundamental truth, you will be immunized against the power of your kid's whining—and much, much closer to ending it.

Next time your kid starts whining, take a deep breath and remember your immunization—your little whiner isn't bringing charges against you at The Hague; he just wants something and is choosing to raise a fuss. Paste on a calm, unflappable face (this is a case of "fake it till you make it," but you'll be happily surprised at how quickly the "make it" part comes) and put the situation in words: "I hear you want to watch a video, but the answer is no," "I know you'd like an ice pop, but we're not having ice pops now," "The park is really fun, but I can't take you today," etc. If (when!) he continues to whine, react quickly (delaying your response just teaches him to keep up the whining to get your attention) and tell him, "You're using your whining voice, but I'm all finished listening to that voice. If you want to whine more, you can whine in your room."

It is easy to say this, but following through is what's important. Don't parrot these words, then let your still-whining kid stalk you throughout the house; if necessary, pick him up, deposit him in his room, and tell him firmly but gently, "I'll be ready to listen as soon as you're ready to use your nice voice." You will not damage your kid in some terrible way by refusing to listen to him whine, nor is it a bad thing for your overwrought kid to discover that he's no longer allowed to inflict his crankiness on the entire household. (He may, in fact, grow to appreciate having his own space to mope around and whine in—I freely confess that I enjoy it from time to time myself.) You will actually hurt your kid far more by engaging with him when he sulks and fusses—that is, by rewarding inappropriate behavior and teaching him that being obnoxious gets results.

This plan will not end the whining immediately; but it will make whining significantly less attractive to your kid, and assuming you encourage his less irritating attempts to make known his feelings and desires, he will soon realize that whining is so last year and adjust his behavior accordingly. But until this awesome day arrives, please keep yourself immunized and standing strong; I am deeply sorry to share that one slip ("Fine! Here's the cookie. Now please stop whining") will require you to start All. Over. Again.

YOUR KID BITES

◆ ◆ ◆ ◆ ◆ ◆ ◆ ◆

When my son was three years old, he came home from preschool with a bite on his leg. Not an ant bite, but actual human teeth marks that reportedly belonged to a two-year-old classmate whom I'll call Simon (because that was his name). Simon, I was told by my son's teacher, was "having a hard time" adjusting to a new baby at home and was expressing his frustration by biting others. This news was delivered in a matter-of-fact tone vaguely infused with sympathy for Simon; of course, I was expected to agree, children bite when they are upset. Faced with an infant sister presumably much more adorable than his bitey little self, why shouldn't Simon be soothed by chomping my son's thigh?

Well, because you can't go around biting people all the time, for one. What might appear an understandable and even reasonable—for a two-year-old, anyway—response when you are the biter's family comes off as more like, oh, I don't know, a possibly actionable assault when you are related to the bitee. There are certainly times most of us would not mind hauling off and slugging someone because they've annoyed us, or simply because we're in a bad mood, but we manage to restrain ourselves and your kid should learn to do so as well.

And just as smacking somebody across the face might make us feel better in the very short term but won't actually help us overcome whatever is bothering us deep down, your kid derives absolutely zero benefit from being allowed to bite with impunity. If your kid is expressing herself by biting, it means she is going through some pretty tough shit. And as much as you might like to imagine that you can shield your kid from experiencing fear, frustration, rage, and all those other unpleasant emotions, the fact is you can't. It's normal for children—even and maybe especially very young children—to feel this way from time to time; and it's up to you, i.e., the adult, to teach your kid to deal with it without drawing blood.

How? First, stop the biting. If your kid sinks her teeth into somebody else's skin, react immediately and strongly and unpleasantly. A bit of drama will serve you well—a horrified gasp, an extremely loud "no," an abrupt and disorienting removal from whatever fun in which your kid had heretofore been participating. Assuming you are not descending into shrill hysterics or physically manhandling your child, don't worry that she will be made unhappy by the proceedings; you are trying to sever the association between biting and an-easy-way-to-let-off-some-steam-and-get-some-enjoyable-attention, so that is actually the goal here.

Once your kid realizes that biting is going to create at least as many problems as it solves, you can do the tougher work of finding out what is really troubling her and helping her deal more appropriately—and effectively—with her emotions. A warning: This may be harder on you than it is on her. After all, parents want children to be happy and innocent, experiencing nothing but sunshine and dancing butterflies and locally sourced organic produce. The realization that your kid is on to the fact that the world sort of sucks is a painful moment. It may seem easier to bypass that moment and let your kid munch a pal rather than say, "Sometimes people bite when they feel sad. Even though it's not okay to bite, it's okay to feel sad. Let's talk about it. When I feel sad, asking for a hug helps me a lot." But refusing to acknowledge that your kid gets mad or scared or just plain down doesn't make those feelings go away; it simply means that instead of teaching her less injurious and more constructive coping mechanisms, you're effectively consigning her to becoming a habitual biter. Which is a rotten thing to do to a kid, even one whose saliva is dripping down my kid's gouged forearm. I mean, yuck.

So what can you do instead? First, teach your kid to match up her feelings with words. Instead of trying to distract her from or coax her out of darker emotions, name them—"I said no when you asked for another cup of juice. You look really angry," or "You must feel frustrated when I have to stop reading to you and take care of the baby"—and encourage her to do the same. Putting a name to the unfamiliar, scary sensations swirling around inside her is empowering for your kid; and if she can trust you to take her seriously and respond when she says, "I'm mad" or "I'm frustrated," she will in time learn to express her emotions with speech rather than teeth.

And yes, I'm aware that talking it out is not always the best solution for an overwrought toddler or preschooler. But there is an awfully long continuum between heart-to-heart chat and cuspids-to-skin chomp, and surely one of the many nonviolent options along that line will resonate with your kid. Try setting up a yell corner where she can retreat and holler to her heart's content when the mood strikes (preferably in a room with a door that closes), give her an old pillow to batter and hit, or keep on hand a "mad pad" and colored pencils where she can draw her angry feelings. As your kid gets older, she may even want to share and explain her "mad pad" art after she calms down—which can provide a possibly unsettling but still pretty awesome glimpse into her psyche and emerging personality.

Need I add a postscript that you should never join the ranks of idiot parents who earnestly advise you that the best way to curb your children's biting is to "bite them back"? I mean, what the fuck? This is the sort of betrayal that may lie dormant for years, then resurface when young Miranda, no longer so young, is deciding whether you will live out your remaining days in the two- or the four-star nursing home. Don't risk it.

YOUR KID SCREAMS

◆ ◆ ◆ ◆ ◆ ◆ ◆ ◆

The exact point at which a baby's happy cry—evoking smiles from nearby strangers and reminiscences about how adorable their own little ones sounded back in the day—becomes a youngster's ear-splitting yell is a bit hazy, but chances are great that your kid has made the transition. This regrettable fact is not difficult to confirm; of course an occasional curmudgeon who hates children will give your kid the stink eye just for breathing audibly or informing you that she has to use the potty (you go, girl!), but if people around your kid are regularly rolling their eyes, sighing loudly, or wincing just about every time she opens her mouth, it may be time for her to pipe down.

I realize this is an unpleasant revelation, likely to be met not with an earnest desire to improve the lot of those within earshot of your kid but with irritation and denial, so let's take a second and talk (quietly!). Of course your kid needs to communicate, and of course it's hard for little ones to regulate their volume, and of course when she gets excited or anxious or has Something Important to say, she might lose a bit of whatever fragile self-control she has managed to develop—I understand all these things, and—believe it or not—most of the people rapidly losing patience with your small yeller do as well. But what they might also recognize is that you have a role to play here, and that role is not to denigrate reasonable people who enjoy relative serenity and quiet but to introduce your kid to basic social mores and the limits of self-expression.

This is a tall order—but it's an essential one. Kids are by nature self-centered, aware of and concerned solely with their own needs, and that's as it should be. They further learn from us, through our loving voices and words and actions, that they are special and important. That's also as it should be. However, everybody is somebody's kid—even the aforementioned stink-eyed curmudgeon—and entitled to have their desires and needs considered as well. Teaching your kid to lower her voice in a public place is perhaps your first opportunity to teach her respect for others and our common humanity. Another tall order, yes—but another essential one.

First, cast off your worries that little Sofia's sense of self will be irretrievably damaged if she is informed that she can't speak whenever, wherever, and at any volume she wishes—if you think about it, you are already compromising her autonomy every time you instruct her to ride in a car seat and poop in a potty, and from where I sit she looks none the worse for wear. Don't fret about stifling her creativity, either; do you remember how in the *Little House* series, Laura Ingalls wasn't allowed to raise her voice, and look how many books she went on to write. Really, your kid will be okay.

Now to instill—and practice—the value of not being a screamer.

The ideal time to embark upon this venture is not at a restaurant or (eek) an airplane; it's something best begun at home, maybe during an afternoon when you are looking for something to do with your kid that does not involve another reading of *Fox in Socks* or disastrous session of finger painting. Tell your kid you have a new game for her, and it's called Loud and Quiet.

It's pretty simple: When you say "loud voice!" your kid gets to be loud, and when you say "quiet voice," she has to get quiet. (I know it sounds kind of dumb, but your kid will like the game, and it really works!) Play the game a lot, but for limited chunks of time so she doesn't get bored or start trying to change the rules. Once she's mastered Loud and Quiet, kick it up a notch and relate the game not just to places she's familiar with—Grandma's house, the zoo, the bank—but also specific situations—playtime at home, the movie theater, the park when you're alone, the park when a couple of adults are chatting nearby. If she's old enough to match up these elements with "loud voice" and "quiet voice" by herself, that is great; if not, no worries—you can tell her which voice goes with which setting. Try switching quickly from "your swing set" to "driving in the rain" to "Mommy has a splitting headache and is out of Advil" and see how fast she can change vocal gears; or let her be the one to call out "loud voice!" and "quiet voice"—and correct you when you (purposely) get them mixed up.

The amazing thing about this game—as you have hopefully already grasped—is that it's so practical! By the time you're heading to a spot that requires a quiet voice, your kid will already know what to expect—and feel good about fulfilling those expectations. Just cue her briefly: "We're going to the library to return our books and for story time. It's time for your quiet voice." No long-winded explanations, no play-by-play instructions. A quick aside, and you're ready to roll.

If you are wondering when I'm going to drop this Loud and Quiet thing and get to talking about the inside and the outside voice—well, I'm not. I know it may seem appealing to join the hordes of parents desperately hissing, "Remember your inside voice, sweetie! Your inside voice!" as their spawn run screeching through the aisles of Target—but even if you have witnessed this technique actually work (which I highly doubt, unless large amounts of candy also traded hands), the simple fact is that Loud and Quiet is so supermuch better. Why? Because while teaching your kid the difference between an outside voice and an inside voice may in fact keep her from yelling in your house, it does the rest of the world no good at all if we happen to be enjoying the beauty of nature when your kid's outside voice happens by. Telling her to switch to her quiet voice is a lot simpler than trying to explain that, well, yes, she may be outside but she still has to stop screaming because there are a lot of people enjoying the beach today and every single one of them wishes she would just shut up.

And the image of the screaming kid does inspire a question: What happens when your kid decides that following the lessons of Loud and Quiet is not as appealing as debuting her loud voice in a quiet voice environment? Don't respond by shouting, "Don't shout!"—you'll look kind of stupid, plus hearing the words "don't shout" actually makes your kid think even more about shouting. Rather, quickly remove her from the area, and calmly remind her that she needs to use her quiet voice—and that there will be consequences for not doing so: "We're at the grocery store, so you need to use your quiet voice. If you switch to your quiet voice, we can finish shopping and finger paint" (ick) "when we get home. If you keep using your loud voice, we will go home and you will lose [insert favorite toy, plan, or privilege] for the day." If she complies, great; if not, grab whatever items you can't live without and get out of there fast. You may fear you're rewarding her for her misbehavior—if, for example, she hates the grocery store and learns that her loud voice is a ticket out—which is why it's crucial that you follow through on the promised consequence. If yelling leads to a premature exit from the store and a session of finger painting anyway because you feel mean denying her, you can be certain she'll yell again; if it leads to a premature exit from the store and a disappointing afternoon, it won't be long before she gets with the program.

Before I hand you your Loud and Quiet–indoctrinated kid, let me add that it's not all about the Quiet. While using her quiet voice in the correct settings and situations is superimportant, it's also superimportant that your kid have time and space and encouragement to be loud. Give her plenty of opportunities to scream and sing and make all kinds of noise—not only will she grow up happy and confident and expressive, but hearing your own kid screech with joy as she runs around the yard or sing "Old MacDonald" at the top of her lungs is actually one of the nicest sounds of all. Sappy, I know, but totally true.

YOUR KID DEMANDS CRAP IN THE CHECKOUT LINE

◆ ◆ ◆ ◆ ◆ ◆ ◆ ◆ ◆

It's not as if grocery shopping with your kid is ever the most fabulous part of your day—if it is, you either go to a really amazing market or just need to find more meaningful stuff to do with your time. But the experience is rarely worse than when you're approaching the finish line—steering a full cart toward the exit, chatting with your miraculously still-smiling kid, feeling almost certain that you're carrying the purse that has your wallet and not the purse you let your kid stuff with old lipsticks and shiny rocks the day before yesterday. You enter the checkout lane, start unloading your organic kale and Greek yogurt and Double Stuf Oreos (sorry, those are mine), imagining what you'll do once you get home and put your kid down for a nap—and then it happens.

"Mommy! I want *that*!"

You know that voice, and your heart sinks. Brightly you turn away from the conveyor belt and beam at your kid. "Hey, sweetie! Can you help me put the yogurt on the counter?"

Please, do you think your kid is some amateur? He's heard these attempts at distraction before; and if they didn't work the first billion times, they're certainly not going to work today. Lest your hope not be totally extinguished, your kid's volume and pitch rise slightly as he points. "Mommy! I want *that*!" That being a bag of M&M's, a box of Tic Tacs, maybe a package of beef jerky. (I know, what the fuck? True story, though!)

Let's decide how to end this tale:

A. Continue ignoring your kid's increasingly impassioned pleas until he loses it completely and starts howling.

B. Paste on more big smiles and repeatedly remind your kid that he's already had a cookie today, and isn't that enough sugar, honey? until he loses it completely and starts howling.

C. Lose your patience and snap that you're not buying him anything, so stop whining, at which point he loses it completely and starts howling.

D. Realize that choices A through C are inevitable unless you just give your kid whatever the antecedent of "that" might be. Cave to his demand, but feel you might lose it completely and start howling.

It's such a horrible conclusion to what should have been a triumphant outing! If only there were a choice E . . .

But there is! It takes a little work, sure; but taming—and eventually ending—your kid's habit of demanding crap in the checkout line is well within your grasp.

Now, it's not as if getting your kid something at the end of a shopping excursion is really so bad. (After all, don't you feel you deserve a reward for making it through? Why do you think *Us* is stowed in the checkout aisle?) If you genuinely like buying treats for your kid, go for it. But if you are feeling uncomfortable with the sheer amount of junk your kid is eating and/or accumulating, or if your kid is reacting to receiving a candy bar or similar not with grateful excitement but with the nonchalant attitude of a baron accepting tribute (barons do accept tribute, right?), it is probably time for a change.

And it's really the routine of getting a treat, rather than the treat itself, that causes the problem. Surprising your kid with a cookie during a shop, delighting him with a pack of neon modeling clay or small stuffed animal in the midst of a trudge through a big-box store, or rewarding him for extra-cooperative behavior at the grocery by letting him select a candy bar for the two of you to split—these are some of the sweetest and most satisfying perks of parenthood. But all the joy disappears when these gifts come to be expected rather than appreciated and when you begin to feel like you're paying off a bribe rather than connecting with your kid.

So if option E is sounding pretty appealing, get ready to embrace it. Know, however, that choosing E starts before you buckle your kid into the cart, or even into the car for a trip to the store.

First off, don't embark on your excursion unless you're sure your kid is well rested and well fed. Yes, raising a fuss in the checkout line is obnoxious—but really, so is packing a very young child into the car for a major shop when you know he's overdue for nap and snack. Once you're preparing to set out, give your kid a brief, matter-of-fact heads-up about what to expect—especially if he's grown accustomed to option D. Say, "We're going to the market now. I know we've gotten in the habit of getting you a treat in the checkout line, but we're not going to do that today. We'll do something fun together when we get home instead." If he protests, take his objections in stride: "I hear that you'd rather have a treat, but that is not the plan today. If you choose to fuss about it, you still won't get a treat, plus we won't be able to do something fun when we get home."

Once you're at the store, don't belabor the point—but do toss a reminder or two his way, especially as checkout looms. You can do this in a sort of sneaky but very effective fashion the second you enter the checkout aisle; before he's had a chance to look around and note the sudden abundance of candy and tchotchkes, give him a huge smile and say proudly, "You're doing such a super job staying quiet in the line! I'm already getting excited about the fun we'll have as soon as we get home." Now, you and I know that he's not doing a super job on purpose—he was just clueless and possibly within thirty seconds of uttering the first of fifty "I want *that*'s." But he doesn't know we know, and chances are great that your praise will distract him from the crap surrounding him—and inspire him to earn even more positive attention with continued good behavior. I'm telling you, it's win-win.

Except, of course, when your kid doesn't want to play along and mounts a tantrum in the checkout line. These are never fun, but look on the bright side—you're close to the exit! And once he settles down, do remember the plan and don't reward him with the after-shop fun you promised for good behavior. Also don't throw up your hands in defeat and decide that the only way to manage your kid is by giving in to his checkout aisle antics; as overwhelming as his toddler- or preschool-sized will might appear at this moment in time, trust me—it is just going to get bigger and more difficult to control. Steeling yourself against buying your screaming kid a bag of beef jerky now is an excellent investment; it will help both of you learn who's really in charge and to behave accordingly. And while paying for and collecting your groceries as your kid howls for a tube of Mentos is not a hell of a lot of fun, it's about a hundred times better than having a similar battle with your now twelve-year-old over a pair of basketball shoes that for reasons you cannot discern costs more than a day at the spa.

Once your kid has managed a couple of crap-free trips through the checkout line, you can reinforce his success by introducing him to one of the favorite pastimes of parents everywhere: observing and commenting on children who are behaving absolutely atrociously. In addition to being totally fun, this practice serves two excellent purposes. First, it lets your kid realize for himself how hideously unpleasant children whining in the checkout line can be and gives him a sense of pride in having jettisoned this particular aspect of brattiness (more to come!). But even more important, it fosters an awesome esprit de corps between you and your kid—a sense that while some kids may behave a certain way, you and he know better and can hold yourselves to a higher standard.

Of course, your kid won't consciously understand the dynamic you're establishing; but trust me, he will quickly develop—and come to enjoy!—the habit of recognizing insufferable behavior and feeling superior to kids who indulge in it. I know we're not supposed to judge—but come on, we all do it, and why not let your kid in on the excitement, especially when doing so will keep him from screaming for a Push Pop when you're on your last nerve in the checkout aisle? And, unlike the Push Pop, it's the gift that keeps on giving: To this day, some of my favorite parenting moments occur as I'm sliding my card, signing with my electronic pen, gathering my bags—and my kid pokes me in the ribs, discreetly nods in the direction of a screechy kid hollering for a treat two aisles away, and whispers, "Brat."

YOUR KID IS MEAN TO THE DOG

◆ ◆ ◆ ◆ ◆ ◆ ◆ ◆

Can I tell you that when I was pregnant with our first kid, my husband and I harbored a huge fear that we would not like our baby as much as we liked our dog? In my defense, I knew practically nothing about babies, plus our dog was really awesome. Once our kid was born, however, this particular worry disappeared (only to be replaced by a million others, but so it goes), as did much of our attentiveness to and concern for Man's Best Friend.

Of course, this happens all the time, and of course it's completely normal and understandable. Your dog probably didn't need all the attention, toys, and treats you foisted on him in your pre-kid days; and as long as you're walking him regularly and playing with him every now and then, he should be doing just fine in his new role as last-but-still-beloved priority around the house.

Until, that is, your kid reaches a certain age. And until you decide to let her do pretty much whatever she wants to the family pet.

Here are a few examples of what I mean:

The time I visited a friend with young children and noticed that their dog was, well, kind of orange. "Oh, I know," the mom laughed when I commented on Buster's new look, "the kids wanted to paint him this morning."

The time a small visitor to my home wanted to see how many times he could shake his fist and yell "stupid!" at my dog before the dog ran away. (Answer: One. Coincidentally the same number of times the kid was invited back, plus one.)

The time a friend's three-year-old mounted the family dog and somehow coerced her into giving the kid a ride around the room. "She's so gentle!" my friend marveled, presumably about the miserable pet whose ears were being vigorously jerked back and forth by the cackling kid.

People, there is a problem here. Having a pet is a great opportunity for your kid to learn empathy, compassion, friendship, and love—but these virtues are difficult to instill when said pet is the object of manhandling and mistreatment. And while you may feel too overwhelmed dealing with your kid to deal with your pet, and far more interested in keeping your kid out of your figurative hair than keeping her out of your dog's actual hair, you owe it to both child and beast to teach her to treat the family pet with respect and kindness.

Begin by setting a good example. You already know what a great imitator your young kid is—so instead of just modeling checking your phone, putting on lipstick, or cursing at the driver in front of you for going so fucking slow, what is wrong with him, model cheerful and attentive care to your pet. If you don't have a lot of time, or even any, to play with the dog, you can still greet him in a happy voice and talk to him in a friendly way while you're getting dressed, making breakfast, or changing your kid's diaper. When the dog gets underfoot or annoys you, don't berate him or give him a frustrated kick; your kid is totally watching and will learn that the dog can be insulted or hit whenever he displeases her. And be sure your kid is around when you are able to connect with the dog; if she sees you petting, snuggling with, and coaxing licks from your pet, she will want to do the same.

Of course she'll need a bit of guidance in doing the same; even the most loving and well-meaning kid will have trouble grasping the difference between sweetly stroking the dog and rubbing the dog's fur roughly, and totally the wrong way to boot. Encourage your kid to pet the dog gently; take her hand and slowly move it along the dog's flank, murmuring "gentle" as you do. If she rips her hand out of yours and delightedly starts whapping the dog, firmly tell her no, then take her hand and demonstrate "gentle" once again. If the whapping starts up again, quickly take her away from the dog; respond matter-of-factly to any fussing by explaining that she's hurting the dog and is only allowed to touch him gently.

Even if "gentle" is too tough a concept for your kid at this point (although it won't be for long, so try again soon), you can find lots of other ways to involve her in caring for her pet. Drawing pictures to hang over your dog's bed, making simple doggie treats by mixing up some peanut butter and kibble (disgusting, I realize, but she'll love stirring up the gooey mess and your dog will devour it), and occasionally picking out dog toys when you go to the grocery store are all great ways for your kid to show affection for the dog without actually getting too close. As she gets more comfortable interacting properly with the dog, you can invite her to fill his water bowl and even feed him at mealtimes; these are especially good practices as they teach your kid to look after her pet and simultaneously signal to the dog that your kid—though a relatively new and small addition to the home—outranks him in the family pack order.

Instilling these behaviors in your kid not only creates a loving, happy relationship between her and the dog but also fosters a loving, happy relationship between your kid and the rest of the world. Think about it: Learning to treat her dog gently will lead to your kid's treating all the members of her family gently, and being admonished for touching the dog roughly may teach her not to touch you roughly, either (which may in turn spare you from being one of the hapless, bruised parents described in the following chapter). Your kid's learning to leave the dog alone when he runs off or takes cover under the bed will correspond to her respecting boundaries and personal space—a lesson better taught now than when she's a tween and routinely barging through your closed bedroom door to help herself to your awesome new boots. Learning to be considerate of her dog will remind your kid to watch out for others less powerful than she—an excellent habit to cultivate if you're entertaining the idea of having another kid, or even taking your current kid to family reunions, fast-food playgrounds (eek), or other places where she'll encounter smaller children.

And when your kid doesn't quite fulfill these expectations? Then it's time to step up, correct her, and make sure she does better. It's good for your kid to see you defending someone who is being hurt; she might be too young to realize consciously that you will do the same for her, but it will still reinforce her growing sense of you as an actively caring and compassionate person. And don't be afraid to reprimand your kid, okay? That's good for her, too, and no, it won't damage her self-esteem. She already knows you love her more than you love the dog, believe me.

But teaching your kid to care for her dog is actually just the beginning. Learning to treat a pet with respect and kindness can be like a gateway drug, but in a good way; it's an introduction to the beauty and the joy of the natural world, and to your kid's responsibility to nurture and protect other living things. And unfortunately, that's not a lesson every kid gets.

While we may cherish the image of kids living in harmony with nature—contentedly playing in the dirt, eagerly watering flowers, watching speechless (ha) and wonderstruck as a flock of geese soars overhead—we also know that's only part of the story. We're also well acquainted with those rampaging children who routinely rip leaves and flowers from their stems, chase birds, throw stuff at squirrels, and delight in stomping on bugs, destroying anthills, and tormenting slugs with sticks. Really, people, even if you despise cockroaches and have traumatic memories of being pooped on by a bird in front of your sniggering third grade car pool (wait, that was me), please do not let your kid engage in these detestable antics. I am not saying it will turn your kid into a serial killer, but I am saying that—well, it's not good. If you don't believe me, ask the mom of the kid who painted the dog orange what her kid was up to just a few years later—and if she doesn't answer, "Shooting frogs with his BB gun at eleven o'clock at night while the friend he'd invited for a sleepover cowered inside the house," I can personally attest she is not telling you the entire truth.

YOUR KID BEATS YOU UP

◆ ◆ ◆ ◆ ◆ ◆ ◆ ◆

Don't let your kid smack you around.

I can say this in a snarky way, providing examples of cowed parents submitting to their toddler's fists. I can repeat what you probably tell your kid every time he whacks you: Hitting isn't *nice*. I can even sympathize with your uncertainty about handling the surprisingly passionate outbursts of rage that pour forth from your very young child.

I can do all these things—and I will. But the message really comes down to seven simple yet searing words: Don't let your kid smack you around.

Let's start with the promised examples: The time I heard odd thwacking noises emanating from my sitting room, where Dad X was ostensibly helping his small son put on his shoes to conclude what Kid X apparently thought was an awesome playdate; the thwacks turned out to be the kid slapping his father every time Dad X got too close with the Skechers Street Lightz. (May I just point out the irony that the shoes contained no leather and were therefore cruelty free?) The time I had dinner with new acquaintances whose kid reacted to being denied a third roll by calmly turning to his mother and socking her in the mouth. The time my friends and I fretted about a woman in our Mommy and Me group who routinely showed up scratched or bruised; we were (mostly) relieved to learn that the injuries had been inflicted not by a brutal spouse but by an ill-tempered three-year-old.

I totally wish these were isolated incidents, episodes I could attribute to bad-seed kids or lousy parents—but you and I both know this shit happens all the time, and if you are reading this chapter, it probably happens to you.

Having your cherished kid whip his precious little hand back and slap you across the face, aim his adorable kid-sized Vans slip-ons that took you forever to find at Nordstrom and kick you in the knee, or narrow his beautiful eyes into slits and rake his nails across your arm is one of the most traumatic parenting moments you will ever experience. As awful as it may be, however, the episode does not mean your kid is a bad kid or that you are a bad parent. I realize this nugget of sympathy may come as a surprise, as much of this book is devoted to my ranting at you, but I really mean it: Every kid experiences frustration, anger, disappointment, and rage; and at some point, almost every kid expresses these dark emotions physically. This means that just about every person you have ever encountered—your favorite teacher, your amazing chiropractor, even the angelically behaved little girl in your kid's preschool class who was potty trained at, like, age one and never throws her snack across the room—probably hauled off and smacked a parent at some point during their early years. (Even one of my kids did, though I won't tell you which.)

Realizing how widespread the behavior is, however, doesn't make it any less horrifying. Seeing a young kid whaling on his parent—and feeling a young kid whaling on his parent, when the parent happens to be you—is really, really shocking. How far will this go? you wonder. How much damage is this tiny kid going to do? And—as the attack continues, and the kid perhaps lands a lucky punch (like a preschooler I know who nearly dislocated his mom's jaw)—how is it going to stop?

Here are the answers: It will go as far as the kid can take it—until he exhausts himself, accidentally hits himself and starts crying (at which point you will make the ironic switch from victim to comforter), or is stopped by a greater force. He will do as much damage as he's permitted to do. And (yes, I'm going back into rant mode now) it is not going to stop if you resort to any of these common responses:

1. You let your kid inflict his worst and wait out the attack.

2. You attempt to calm your small assailant by sweetly asking why he's angry and reminding him to use his words (a nifty bit of multitasking, as you're simultaneously dodging a flurry of blows).

3. You force a laugh and act as if what's transpiring is no big deal.

These responses are totally understandable. You've been told a million times that forcing your kid to repress his emotions is unhealthy and harmful, so enduring (more than) a few punches as he expresses frustration and anger seems like part of your parental duty. You know you should remain patient and accepting at all times, and ignoring the smacks while trying to placate your kid with love and tenderness sounds like what a truly devoted parent would do. You know you're supposed to appear in control and unflappable at every moment, so you play off the fact that your kid is hurting you, like, a lot. (This last one is a favored reaction when other people are around, but trust me—no one is fooled.)

As understandable as these responses may be, and as earnest and hopeful as you may feel while deploying them, their shortcomings are revealed by the fact that they are not actually doing any good. At the end of the day, your kid is still beating you up—which means it's time to take a deeper look at the situation and explore some new ways to handle it. Let's get started.

Of course your kid gets upset, and of course he's too young to express his angst with the aplomb of a Trent Reznor or a *Jagged Little Pill*–era Alanis Morissette (although he might be able to master the art of emoji—just an idea). Of course you want to encourage your kid to share his feelings—even when those feelings are anger or outrage or fury and his sharing them will make your day far less pleasant. Of course you want to remain even-tempered and serene when your kid is so clearly overwhelmed. However, your job is about more than upholding all these important and awesome convictions—your job is upholding all these important and awesome convictions without turning yourself into your kid's personal punching bag.

And you must start now. Because, far more than whining, far more than screaming, far more than demanding crap in the checkout line and picky eating and lousy sleeping, your kid's beating you up needs to be recognized as the humongously catastrophic disaster that it is.

I sense your skepticism, and if it concerns the fact that "humongously" may not in fact function as an adverb, yes, I defer to you. However, I remain stalwart in my conviction that letting your kid smack you around is one of the worst things you can do as a parent.

Yes, one of the worst things *you* can do. Not that your kid is winning any offspring-of-the-year awards by pounding his fists repeatedly against your cheeks, and not that you're having the time of your life getting clobbered—but believe it or not, the one suffering the most from this onslaught is your knuckle-wielding kid. Because with every smack, your kid is learning that violence is acceptable. He's learning that feeling disappointment, anger, and frustration gives him the right to hurt people who love him. And he's learning that you—his supposedly omnipotent, strong, and protective parent—don't fight back when someone hurts you, and wondering how, if that's the case, he can possibly trust you to keep him safe.

So if you won't stop letting your kid smack you around for your own sake—do it for his.

I hope I have you convinced—because even if you're one hundred percent on board, handling a literal smack-down from your kid is never easy. Even the first step sounds ridiculous, considering that you're being physically harmed by a very small person: Stay strong. Really, stay strong! Remember that you are the parent, you are the adult, and you have the power here. So act like it! Firmly—not painfully, but not half-assedly either—grab your kid's hand or foot or whatever body part he's employing as a weapon, look him directly in the eye, and say in your best don't-fuck-with-me voice (don't pretend you don't know what I'm talking about, everybody's got one), "No. You do not hurt me." Ideally, the strength of your reaction will stun your kid enough that he halts his attack, in which case you can praise him for regaining control and distract him from or deal with whatever set him off.

If, however, your kid barely misses a beat and starts pummeling you with whatever limbs are still free, you need to take more assertive action. As swiftly as possible, immobilize your kid and move to a safe space; as you do so, use your don't-fuck-with-me tone to say something like, "You do not hurt me. It's okay to be angry, but it is never okay to hurt me." Continue holding your kid and repeating these phrases until he settles down; it won't take as long as you think, in part because your strong, steady reaction will help stabilize him. Once the storm passes, calmly tell your kid that sometimes when people get angry, they want to hurt other people, but that he may not hurt you. Your assurance that what he's feeling is normal and that you are strong enough to get him through it will be extremely soothing to your kid—his flying fists are every bit as scary to him as they are to you. A really effective mantra is "I will stop you from hurting me until you can stop yourself"—it's simple, it gets the point across, and it conveys your expectation that your kid will not be pulling this shit forever.

Of course you still need to help your kid process whatever

prompted the attack, and guide him to find more effective ways of dealing with challenging feelings than cuffing his relatives—but honestly, none of that can happen until your kid accepts that you are in control and recognizes that you are tough enough to keep yourself—and therefore him—safe from harm. You will also be amazed at the confidence boost you will draw from this response; you don't realize how draining it is to be physically hurt by your own child until you aren't anymore.

Just a quick P.S. and yet another nugget of sympathy: Chances are overwhelmingly large that your kid is beating you up simply because, well, that's what kids do. However, I have a friend whose sweet-as-sugar kid slapped her across the face—and was truly bewildered to learn that hitting adults wasn't allowed. The kid had witnessed a preschool classmate smack the teacher so many times that she assumed that was the way life worked. So just in case your kid happens to be the other one in a trillion who would never, never, never instigate any aggressive or hurtful behavior on his own, engage in some due diligence to see who or what might be influencing his conduct. And of course take your kid to the pediatrician if he seems truly violent or scares you in any way. I'm almost positive he's fine, but a second opinion—particularly from a medical professional who's actually met your child—can't hurt.

YOUR KID CLINGS

◆ ◆ ◆ ◆ ◆ ◆ ◆ ◆

If you ever doubt that you are a superimportant person and that the universe cannot function properly without you, try walking away from your kid when she appears engrossed in playdough or dot art markers. What seemed to be a happy, carefree child will immediately morph into a howling toddler or preschooler wholly dependent on you for safety, companionship, and a general purpose in life.

Honestly, this is often kind of nice, especially if you are occasionally haunted by those dark nights of the soul that give rise to existential questions like, what am I doing with my rapidly diminishing youth and will I truly leave my mark on this world and does little Evangeline love her mom more than my kid loves me because Evangeline's mom lets her decorate cupcakes all the time? (No, by the way.) Having a person you adore fall apart completely at the prospect of your going to the bathroom alone—well, it feels good. You feel needed and essential and valued. You feel that you and your kid are a team. You feel special.

Of course, there are also a few drawbacks to this situation; and since you are perusing this chapter, I am assuming you have encountered them.

ONE: It's inconvenient and—dare I say—annoying. I realize that using these words to describe your kid's attachment to you sounds a little bit horrible; but really, how else would you characterize the feverish screams that accompany your every attempt to move, like, ten feet away from your kid? Having your kid glued to your side lest she erupt into a terrified tantrum is not the most fabulous prospect in the world, nor is the specter of never again spending five minutes alone. The only positive is that your situation does perhaps offer a taste of a more exciting and glamorous life—say, that of Angelina Jolie, denied privacy and besieged by paparazzi at every turn, except that paparazzi don't drool all over you. Much.

TWO: It causes a lot of guilt. Whether you're hostile to, conflicted about, or totally on board with your kid's determination to be within arm's reach of you every second of every day, at some point her wishes are going to be foiled. It could be work, it could be plans with a friend, it could be the pee that you've already held for three hours and just can't put off any longer—but eventually you are going to walk away from your kid, she is going to freak out, and you are going to feel terrible. Of course parenting is all about guilt, and of course you're making all kinds of horrific mistakes that are sure to doom your kid to expensive therapy for most of her life, but feeling guilty for going to the bathroom just in time to prevent yet another urinary tract infection is a wee bit extreme, in my opinion.

THREE: It really hurts your kid. Not to minimize the unpleasantness of experiencing inconvenience, annoyance, and guilt—they totally suck—but the terror, dread, and panic your kid is enduring are much, much worse. Imagine that you're scuba diving for the first time, and that your breathing apparatus and oxygen tank keep getting up and walking away. This is life for your kid.

So yeah, separation anxiety—my kid's Gymboree facilitator downplayed it as separation "awareness," but come on—is pretty tough. Managing this behavior, however, is a lot different from dealing with whining and biting and crap like that—simply because it's a normal and appropriate part of your kid's development. No matter how frustrating its manifestations may be, separation anxiety is a real thing—and your kid deserves your patience, understanding, and accommodation as both of you get through it.

Patience, understanding, and accommodation, however, are not the same as encouragement. The ultimate goal here is not to establish a new dynamic where your kid controls your every movement and you cripple her ability to thrive in your absence—but to show your kid that you'll come back for her and that she's okay even when you're not around.

I acknowledge that this sentiment is not universally shared.

Please refrain from sending me links to *National Geographic* or whatever else you are ruminating about; I am already well aware that babies in many countries are carried around in slings all the time and accompany their moms into the fields and sleep next to a parent and reportedly lead happy and secure lives literally attached to their devoted mothers, and that people you know may wish to re-create this world for their toddlers and preschoolers. If that sounds like a good plan to you, I wish you a lot of luck and warn you that you might not really like this book.

But wait! Before you hurry off to purchase a custom sling for a forty-five-pound kid (really?), please do take a moment to consider whether this will truly prove an ideal life. Yes, your kid's attachment to you is of central and vital importance. But have some faith in that attachment; it's a lot stronger than you're giving it credit for being, and it's not going to snap if you get your kid out of your hair every now and then. And as important as attachment is, other things are important as well: things like learning to trust, learning that people can leave and come back, learning that there is more than one person who can keep you safe. These, too, are great things to instill in your kid.

And it's not only about your kid. Even as your kid copes with separation anxiety, you are still entitled to have your own interests and your own life. Maybe you do not need to go to extremes, like a mom I know who spent her entire maternity leave getting postnatal massages and eating at fancy restaurants while her nanny kept the baby ("I am so not ready to go back to work tomorrow!" she proclaimed as we sat in my backyard together, she looking totally awesome after some benefit luncheon, I finishing up my kid's abandoned bowl of mac and cheese as he slathered my feet with mud)—but neither should you cancel long-held plans for a girls' night out because your kid started fussing when you handed him off to Dad (another true story, only this time I was the one looking totally awesome, at least until I traded my dress and supercute boots for sweats and spent yet another evening watching *Dora* and quartering grapes. And while, yes, every moment with my family is precious, I should have gone out with my friends).

There are many ways you can impart to your kid the lessons that people go away and come back and that object permanence is totally for real: rounds of peekaboo, games of hide-a-toy-under-a-cushion-and-act-all-excited-when-your-kid-pulls-it-out-again (not superriveting, but actually kind of fun if you are in the mood), books and stories about separating and reuniting. You can also introduce phrases like "Mommy always comes back!" when you leave and return to a room, or get your kid accustomed to holding a particular stuffed animal or lovey while you are away. If these suggestions leave you ravenous for more activities of this type, you seriously need to get out more, but your pediatrician will probably have a few additional ideas.

All this, however, is just prologue; the real action comes when it's time to say good-bye to your screaming kid and head out the door. I am assuming you have screened whoever is staying with your kid, that she and your kid have met each other, and that you have made sure they clicked as much as a grown person and a small kid, even one as advanced and amazing as yours, can possibly click—that's pretty basic, I mean, really. But here's some more stuff you can do in order to make the separation go more smoothly:

ONE: Don't wait until your kid's engaged in play with her sitter, then sneak off without saying good-bye. While this may save you an unpleasant separation, it's kind of an asshole move and can really screw with your kid. Would you like someone you love to do this to you? If so, you have some significant problems; but either way, don't do it to your kid.

TWO: Don't tell your kid good-bye and start to leave, then rush back to comfort her when she begins to fuss. Not only will this bewilder your kid, but it will almost certainly make you late for whatever fabulous engagement you have planned. It also annoys the sitter, and believe me, you want to keep her happy and eager for future employment.

THREE: Put on a serene face. Of course this situation is totally stressing you out, but try not to let your kid know. She won't understand that your anxiety stems from a complex brew of love, guilt, frustration, blah blah blah—she'll just sense that you're even more high-strung than usual and assume you share her skittishness about letting each other out of your sight.

So when it's time to go, just go. Well, don't just go—give your kid a warning and a few minutes to prepare before you head out, then give her a loving, firm, confident good-bye, and then go. Many families have a little good-bye ritual; if this works for you and your kid, that is great, but don't feel you are failing your kid if all she gets is a kiss and hug. Though as you walk out the door (finally!), you might remind your kid that she is safe without you—hearing yourself say it will remind you as well.

And just a note for those of you lucky enough to be hitting the town for a romantic interlude with your partner: Once you've managed to separate from your kid, the only thing standing between you and some fantastic grown-up time is, well, you. So don't blow it! Picking a fight with your partner because you feel guilty about leaving your kid is totally unfair as well as totally ineffective; I have personally ruined several evenings doing this, so I know of what I speak. You're still away from your kid, so you've still got the guilt; you're just miserable now to boot. And probably making the person you're with miserable, too, which is not nice at all. Sorry, honey!

YOUR KID REFUSES TO WEAR ANYTHING EXCEPT HER NIGHTGOWN

◆ ◆ ◆ ◆ ◆ ◆ ◆ ◆

This is the story of my very best friend in the entire world and her amazing and wonderful daughter. This daughter now wears a variety of clothing—but during our earliest encounters, she was dressed in a nightgown. This surprised me at the time, as it was the middle of the day, but I soon learned not to be surprised because Sara was always dressed in a nightgown. A princess nightgown, to be exact—she had two, which meant that whichever one she was not wearing was in the wash, and it had damn well better be clean and dry the second she needed it.

My best friend and I look back on this time with smiles and affectionate memories (also a bit of nostalgia because a princess nightgown beats the hell out of most clothing ensembles available to tween girls today), but at the time, oh my gosh, it was really stressful. Not only the daily laundry, which definitely sucked in and of itself, but also and especially Sara's stubborn insistence on wearing those particular articles of clothing every single moment. It seemed so important to her, so fundamental to her identity, so central to her whole being—you seriously wondered what permanent damage would be wrought on her three-year-old psyche if she were forced to wear something else.

Years later, I am convinced that—handled properly—it would have been totally and completely fine. And although it is too late for us, I hope this revelation will come in time to save you a million loads of laundry—and to help you begin instilling in your kid the values of flexibility and equanimity.

I realize these are lofty words—and a lofty goal—for your very young kid. And at first they seem not to fit at all. After all, your kid is struggling with so much already. She's just coming to grips with the fact that she's a separate and discrete being, she's simultaneously craving independence and terrified to exercise it, she's adrift in a sea of physical and emotional changes and desperately seeking a sense of safety and control—under the circumstances, shouldn't you understand and indulge her demand to wear a particular nightgown, have her books stacked a particular way, or eat all her meals on one particular plate?

Well, no. Because as much as these practices may placate your kid in the short term, they actually subvert your long-term goal—which is to help her transition from wholly dependent infant to semiautonomous individual in a healthy, functional way. Wearing the same nightgown every day or being served every breakfast, lunch, dinner, and snack on the same plate gives your kid a sense of control, sure—but it also makes her world very rigid, very narrow, and very unstable. If your kid falls apart at the prospect of leaving the house in a different outfit, or refuses to eat food presented on a different plate, it's tough to argue that she's really being helped by adhering to these rituals.

Nor is it just about your kid: Unless you cherish the extra labor and anxiety that her dependence on these rituals brings you (and if you do, please come to my house—I have ten loads of laundry and a sink full of dishes, and you are welcome to have at it), they're not doing anything positive for you, either. This is no small consideration, because the dynamic you're setting up with your kid will endure long after she's passed through these developmental stages. Acquiescing to her three-year-old demands in order to give her a sense of security will—all too quickly and probably without your realizing it—morph into your acquiescing to her six-, seven-, and eight-year-old demands in order to stave off a tantrum. Which is a dynamic you definitely Do. Not. Want.

So how do you break these habits? With gentleness and understanding, of course—but also with firmness and confidence. It's best to launch this plan on a day when you have some flexibility; things will go infinitely better if you're not under pressure to have your kid fed, dressed, and out the door at some particular time. Begin by giving your kid a heads-up that the change is coming—"Your egg is almost ready, and you'll have the green plate today," or "It's almost time to get dressed, and you'll need to wear a regular outfit today"—but follow through without apology or lengthy commentary. If she reacts badly—which, I'm sorry to say, she almost certainly will—empathize with how she's feeling without backing down: "I know there are only a couple of things you like to wear and that wearing them is important to you. But you are safe no matter what you wear. I can choose an outfit for you, or we can go to your closet and choose it together." If she continues to carry on, tell her calmly, "It looks as if I'll need to choose your clothes for you"—this may be enough to stanch the tears; and if she pulls herself together enough to select a new outfit, give her a wide berth in doing so (this would not be the day to insist on matching colors or complementary patterns, for example).

Of course you can be (somewhat) flexible in implementing this new dynamic. Feel free to give your kid a couple days of advance warning before actually switching her plate or requiring a non-nightgown-related outfit, for example, or to start a sticker chart or marble jar to reward cooperation. You may also want to plan a meal she especially likes or a trip to her favorite playground to make the prospect of using a different plate or wearing a different outfit more appealing—as well as to dissuade her from going all nonviolent resistance and simply refusing to eat or dress.

Remember: The point of all this is ultimately to help both of you navigate her transition from little kid to bigger kid and to set acceptable parameters in which she can exercise her legitimate need for security and control. It's not about teaching her to "grow up, already!" or "be a big girl!" or telling her, "Put away your binky—you're too old for that!" (If you think I'm getting in the middle of the argument you're having with your spouse or in-laws about whether your kid is too old for a pacifier or bottle, by the way, you are seriously deluded. I will go out on a limb, however, and suggest that maybe whatever binky-related activities happen in the big-girl bed should stay in the big-girl bed.) Calmly repeating that you understand your kid is upset, reminding her that she is safe, and trying to engage her in other activities will go a much longer way than shaming or scolding. And while of course you should not allow your kid to throw endless tantrums over these changes, neither should you dismiss the feelings of genuine anxiety and uncertainty that lie at the heart of her behavior.

Be sure, too, to offer your kid plenty of other opportunities to achieve the security and control she's seeking. Of course it's much easier—and much, much less time-consuming—to put your kid's shoes on her feet for her, to pour her milk, to wash her hair, to zip up her jacket, to schlep her around in the stroller. But if your kid is yearning to do more for herself, you've got to relax your schedule a bit and let her try. Mastering the elusive shoelace and zipper, figuring out how to pour liquid so it actually goes in the cup, shampooing and rinsing, venturing out of the stroller and pushing it for a little while: These are all age-appropriate ways for your kid to build skills, gain confidence, and feel empowered. And, unlike donning a special nightgown or lining up the food in her play kitchen exactly-like-that, these practices will help her develop an authentic sense of rootedness, safety, and autonomy.

Believe it or not, you are actually helping not just your future kid but also your present kid by easing her reliance on these rituals. As difficult as it will be for her to end her monogamous relationship with a certain outfit, plate, arrangement of toys, or whatever, it will also be a relief. At some point, the security of a routine and the reassurance associated with a particular object morph into something unhealthy and unhelpful; and if you felt the need to read this chapter, your kid has probably reached that point. You are doing much more than expanding her wardrobe and choice of tableware; you are also liberating her from an increasingly cramped comfort zone and enabling her to find a sense of safety—and a sense of self—in the wider world. You are also teaching your kid that she can function even when the world is not operating exactly as she might like and helping her face change and the unexpected with confidence and composure.

It may be hard to remember all this when your kid's screaming for a nightgown or dumping her food off the new plate, but hold fast, because I promise it's totally true. I can also (almost) promise that she won't remember these episodes as traumatic or painful; just ask my son, who as a toddler nearly drove me insane with his insistence on wearing his pants rolled up to midthigh, even when it was literally freezing outside—and who has no recollection of the tantrum and tears that accompanied the breaking of this habit. "Remember when I used to wear my pants the wrong way?" he'll ask offhandedly these days, usually while reaching for my phone. "I was so weird."

YOUR KID WILL EAT ONLY THREE THINGS

◆ ◆ ◆ ◆ ◆ ◆ ◆ ◆

Here's a news flash: If your kid gets hungry enough, he'll eat.

I'll say it louder, because this is truly amazing and important news, and you can't possibly hear it over your anguished cries as you beg little Ethan to take another bite of chicken nugget, please, please, honey, just one more: If your kid gets hungry enough, he'll eat.

Now on the heels of this news flash, here's a disclaimer: If your kid has genuine medical issues, of course I am not talking to you. But if you are blessed with a generally healthy, active kid who is simply too busy yanking the pillows off your couch or wiping his snot on the cat to sit in the high chair and eat a proper meal, well, then yeah, read on. Ditto if you feel certain your kid's famished but he's furiously rejecting every edible you place in front of him because he suspects (rightly) that at the end of this foodstuff parade lies a bowl of plain pasta and a tube of SpongeBob Strawberry Riptide Go-Gurt.

I know the urge to feed our kids is one of the strongest, most primal we've got, certainly more powerful than the urge to put on some foundation and read something more challenging than *Where the Wild Things Are*, awesome though it may be. I also know that it's the rare parent for whom eating is simply about nutrition and enjoyment—for many of us, it's also a harrowing trip back to maybe-not-so-long-ago days when the numbers on the scale determined our self-esteem and when lunch meant Diet Coke and three Babybel cheese wheels (150 calories!). It's totally understandable to equate nurturing your kid with giving in to his every meal-related whim, and to believe that doing otherwise will put him on the path to an unhealthy relationship with food and disordered eating—but it's also totally wrong.

Here's the thing: Not every encounter with food is make-or-break for your kid's future physical and emotional health. And if it were, that would be pretty bad news. Being chased around the living room with string cheese or a fistful of Goldfish; trying to play but being distracted by a parent's desperate pleas to eat a few bites; having permission to shriek and whine when presented with unappealing meals; flinging away food only to have a parent grimly sally forth with a new option; and subsisting on the aforementioned bowl of plain pasta and Go-Gurt every . . . single . . . night because "he just won't eat anything else—he's such a picky eater!"—really, these episodes do not scream "path to positive and wholesome eating habits," you know?

So let's take a deep breath and dare to imagine that a meal is just a meal. That is, you offer your kid some reasonably appealing, nutritious food, he either accepts it or rejects it, and you call it a day.

It's not like he's off to enlist in the merchant marines as soon as you unbuckle him from the booster seat; he'll have the chance to eat again in three hours, and if he gets hungry in the meantime, well, perhaps he'll be a bit more receptive to the perfectly acceptable black bean quesadilla he just hurled to the floor.

Next time your kid's due to eat, begin with a cheerful reminder that it's almost time to get into the high chair for a meal. Don't back down if he balks or fusses; he's still small and portable enough to be picked up and plopped in, so enjoy it while you can. Even if your entire family isn't sitting around the table together, you can provide a regular framework for eating; make it a friendly time by grabbing a seat and having a little nosh yourself, and talk with him about airplanes, farm animals, that accursed SpongeBob—anything besides how much he has consumed and why won't he just try the veggie crisp, just try it, sweetie, it's good, please. Offer small portions of a couple of items he likes (or at least that he liked yesterday, which may not be the same thing)—these can be graham crackers, pieces of fruit, or string cheese, keep it simple—as well as a new food or two you'd like him to sample. Once he finishes up his favorites, don't immediately run to refill his plate; let him consider the interloper and calmly encourage him to try it. If he refuses, gets angry, or starts yelling, throwing food, or engaging in other charming behaviors, don't panic, bargain, or soothe; simply whisk his plate out of reach and say, "I can see you don't like what's on your plate, but this is what we have to eat. If you'd like to calm down and try again, you can have the food back." If you ignore him (or at least muster the acting skills to convince him you can't hear his fussing) and continue eating your own meal, he may in fact settle down and give the food a try. If not, take a few more bites, clear your plate, and tell your kid, "It looks like mealtime is over! As soon as you're quiet, you can get down and play."

Will this work the first time? Of course not! You've been waiting on your kid hand and foot, plying him with dinosaur-shaped chicken nuggets and squeezable fruit and shit, teaching him that he's the boss at mealtimes (and every other time as well, but we'll deal with that in other chapters)—and suddenly you expect him to eat what's placed in front of him and, by the way, to cut out all that ridiculous screaming and carrying on? Ha! But guess what? If you're consistent, calm, and firm; if you involve your kid in meal preparation as much as practically possible (letting him tear lettuce, for example, or pour water from a plastic pitcher); if you remember that a kid may reject a new food a dozen times, then inexplicably sample and love it on the thirteenth try; and if you gird yourself with the image of a toddler gleefully diving into a plate of hummus and tabbouleh (true story, though not about my kid, regrettably)—well, it won't be long before your kid realizes there's a new sheriff in town. And this sheriff (yes, I mean you) doesn't traffic exclusively in food that comes wrapped in plastic, remains serene (at least outwardly) in the face of meal-related tantrums, and recognizes that the correct adult response to a kid's picky eating is not trotting off to prepare the three foods he's standing up in his booster seat braying about, but getting said kid to sit down and eat what's in front of him.

In the short term, I know it's oh-so-much easier just to go along with the picky eating, to prepare a separate meal for your kid and comfort yourself that he'll grow out of it—but for the sake of your future self, please reexamine that scenario. A three-year-old who's allowed to determine his diet—and to make his food preferences known by yelling about and tossing aside whatever doesn't please his palate—is unlikely to morph into the easygoing, go-with-the-flow, "sure, I'll try some of that, thanks" kid you're envisioning. And even if he does (he won't!), you'll make yourself anxious, miserable, and stressed during the intervening years, which is really not fair to you at all. Honestly, you do quite enough for your kid—don't you deserve to drop the Goldfish and sit back while he plays, to prepare just one meal for everyone to eat (or not) as they choose, and to get through dinnertime without having to scrub spurned spinach quiche from your wall?

And while you're still strapped into your figurative high chair, please indulge me in a brief word about snacks:

Yes, I am well aware that your kid needs a snack—hell, I could use a snack myself, and I ate a rather large lunch just two hours ago. But snacks can be a huge stumbling block to reforming your picky eater. If your kid rejects his breakfast but receives a granola bar and piece of fruit leather ninety minutes later, well, you can hardly blame him for learning to forgo meals and get his daily nutrition, such as it is, at snack time. Rather, use snacks to reinforce the eating habits you're trying to instill. For example, a hungry kid allowed to choose among orange slices, carrot sticks, or nothing for snack is not very likely to choose nothing. At least, not after he's learned to take you seriously—and maybe even developed a taste for tabbouleh.

YOUR KID IS A LOUSY SLEEPER

◆ ◆ ◆ ◆ ◆ ◆ ◆ ◆

This chapter is titled "Your Kid Is a Lousy Sleeper," but honestly, there is no possible way your kid is as lousy a sleeper as mine was. I am not trying to goad you into a round of "Let's Complain About Our Kids and See Who's the Most Miserable"—I am just stating a fact.

Want proof? The second day of my kid's life, I let the nurse take him for a few hours so I could get some rest. (Yes, I had spent, like, every minute up to that point cuddling him, and yes, I'd just breastfed him into a state of contended drowsiness, so leave me alone.) It was the middle of the night, and I was exhausted and figured he was, too. After about thirty minutes, just as I was drifting off into desperately needed slumber, I heard a faint noise from down the hall. It sounded like a crying baby. That poor mom, I thought hazily. I'm so glad my kid is dozing happily in the nursery. Then the noise got louder. Wow, I thought, that mom should shut the door. Then it got even louder. Then it stopped Right. Outside. My. Room.

"I'm sorry," the nurse said, not looking at all sorry to turn my screaming, no-longer-contentedly-drowsy baby back over to me. "He just won't go to sleep."

Along with being wonderful and adorable in every way, this became my kid's defining characteristic: He just wouldn't go to sleep. When he'd cry at two a.m., it got so that I just started waking up for the day, knowing that was the end of my rest for the night. I burned off much of my leftover pregnancy weight walking him in endless circles around the house, vainly attempting to lull him into a slumber that would last longer than ten minutes if I dared to put him down. It is sort of funny now, but it wasn't then—it was hard and awful and occasionally terrifying. And if you are thinking that you know better, that if only I'd tried this, or if I'd just read that book, seriously, shut up. I tried it all, I read it all, and none of it worked.

I tell you this because—well, in part because I'm clearly still trying to process those months of my life, but mostly because I want you to know that I get it. There is little more annoying than the parent of a kid who has slept through the night since month one handing out advice, unless that advice is "Get lucky and hope your luck holds with kids two and three" (it won't)—and I am not that parent. I am, however, a parent who managed to create an excellent sleeper out of raw material that was, shall we say, less than promising. And you can do the same.

You and I are both aware that my name on this book cover is not preceded by "Dr.," nor followed by "PhD" or "certified sleep specialist," if such a thing even exists, which it should. So I am not going to pretend to be qualified to provide a step-by-step guide for teaching an infant to sleep through the night, or to evaluate studies that one side claims as proof that sleep training will render a kid incapable of ever forming positive attachments with another living being and that another side claims as proof that sleep training promotes a kid's brain development, logical thinking, and regulation of emotions. I will say, however, that, while leaving a two-month-old to cry himself to sleep is totally barbaric, letting a ten-month-old with a full belly and dry diaper summon his parent to his bedside every thirty minutes night after night is not an ideal situation, either. And if you happen to be the parent of that ten-month-old, and you and your pediatrician agree that the best way to change this nighttime dynamic is some sort of sleep training, you do not owe anyone an apology or explanation. Seriously, I am one of the most judgy people around; and if I am not judging you, no one should.

The problem is that lousy sleeping persists far longer than you might realize. By the time your kid is a toddler or preschooler, you're likely to answer the question "Is your kid a good sleeper?" with an enthusiastic yes—especially as you recall those endless nights of feeding and soothing and changing that ended not all that long ago. But consider the question a bit more deeply, and you might say, well . . . yes . . . except.

Except your kid requires your presence in his bed in order to fall asleep, right? Except for five requests for glasses of water and monster checks every night? Except for three a.m. visits to your room? Except for rejecting the prospect of a midday nap despite clearly being really, really tired?

Now, you might be so relieved that your kid is no longer glued to your boob for five hours a night—or screaming whenever you try to lay him down in the crib and take your boobs back to bed—that you are willing to live with these "excepts." But the "excepts" take a toll, on your kid as well as on you, and it's time to resolve them.

Whether he's imagining monsters, clambering into your bed in the middle of the night, or refusing to go to sleep without you, your kid is dealing with really common, age-appropriate issues: He's both delighted with and terrified of his burgeoning independence and maturity, and he's not sure he's entirely safe without you once the lights dim. And while it might seem more supportive (not to mention easier) to give in to his demands, you'll actually help your kid—and yourself—a lot more by standing strong.

Here's an example of what I mean: Say your kid is fussing about monsters in the closet. You do what good parents are supposed to do—you whip out a water bottle you've colorfully labeled "Monster Spray," give the closet a spritz or two, and inform him the monsters have been scared away. In the short term, yeah, this is an awesome solution: Your kid's fear is assuaged, and you can duck out of his room and finish watching *Orange Is the New Black*. But in the long term, not so much. Rather than assuring him that monsters are not real and exploring what the monsters represent to him—that is, what's really frightening him—you've just reinforced your kid's belief that he's not safe in his room and that only you can keep the dangers at bay. Ditto for lying down with your kid until he falls asleep every night, offering your kid a season pass to your bed, or joining your kid on the couch for yet another viewing of *Rio 2* instead of putting him down for a much-needed snooze because he tearfully insists he doesn't want to nap. All these responses—all these "excepts"—play into your kid's anxieties rather than enabling him to overcome them.

So what should you do instead? First, talk honestly and openly with your kid. Now, I realize that discussing fears and anxieties and emotions with a young kid is not the easiest thing in the world, but it's easier than waiting until he's in elementary school to kick him out of your bed (more on that later) and much more gratifying to boot. Find a neutral time during the day and gently ask your kid about the monsters in his closet or his apprehension about falling asleep on his own or his nervousness about being in his room alone at night. What do the monsters look like? What else scares him? Why does he feel safe when you are with him? Invite him to respond with words, with drawings, with his toys acting out his replies—whatever feels best to him. Once your kid opens up—and he will, if you show that you are genuinely interested in and taking seriously what he has to say—you will be amazed at how much your kid has considered these matters and at the glimpse into his psyche and his inner life that his answers will provide. This conversation will accomplish more than a hundred bottles of monster spray in helping your kid cope with what is truly bothering him; and once you understand the sources of his angst, you can guide him through it not with gimmicks but in a meaningful, appropriate way.

You can also help your kid develop happier feelings about his bed. This may sound ridiculous, especially when you know bed is, like, the best place in the world; but right now your kid sees his bed as a scary enemy, a place of loneliness and powerlessness. By making bed a welcoming and fun place—by reading your kid's favorite stories or playing his favorite games on it during the day, for example, or even serving a favorite snack on it if you can abide the mess—you make the prospect of staying in bed all night significantly more appealing.

Of course, not every second of this process will be sharing and warmth. The moment will still arrive when you walk out of the room at bedtime and leave your kid behind, or you firmly escort him back to his own bed when he crawls into yours during the night. Knowing that you're dealing with the real issues behind these behaviors will make the moments easier, but they'll still kind of suck. They'll go much better, however, if you remain firm and matter-of-fact; wavering on the rules you've previously set, or giving in just because your kid seems so upset, will actually worsen the situation by making your kid wonder if you, too, doubt that he's really safe in his bed. You might ease the transition by rewarding your kid for staying in bed all night or by giving him a new security object that he can use to remind himself everything's okay—but do prepare yourself for some tough nights until your kid adjusts to the new routine.

Even with these nights of, shall we say, compromised rest, it really will not be long before you and your kid are on a better, sleepier path. The change will be good for him—as much as he may resist it, your kid needs sleep; and you will notice major improvements in his mood, behavior, and even abilities as he gets more of it. He'll also learn to self-soothe and to recognize and regulate his own sleep needs—pretty awesome skills for a kid still young enough not to find *Rio 2* totally annoying. And once you are putting your kid to bed at a reasonable time, and passing a couple of pleasantly kid-free hours before trundling off to sleep yourself, you will probably notice some improvements in your own mood as well.

If you're balking, rationalizing that your kid is too small and tender to brave the night hours on his own—well, let me share this cautionary tale: A mom friend of mine who felt that way, and who in fact loudly and passionately made known her convictions every time the subject was broached, ended up realizing far too late that her no-longer-small-and-tender kid needed to fall asleep without her by his side and to finish up his sleep somewhere besides her husband's place in the marital bed. By then, her kid was old enough (five and a half!—but who's counting?) to concoct all sorts of sneaky tricks to escape his own bed and displace his dad—to the point that my friend spent many sleepless nights crouched on the floor of her own bedroom, frantically wedging a chair under the door handle so her kid could not get inside. Eventually, yes, her kid learned to fall asleep on his own—but wait and see, he is going to make some lucky therapist very rich someday.

YOUR KID ANNOYS STRANGERS

◆ ◆ ◆ ◆ ◆ ◆ ◆ ◆

Has this happened to you? I cannot be the only one.

Spending a couple of hours away from my own offspring, I head to a café that is clearly not kid friendly: There is no children's menu touting mac and cheese, no stack of high chairs, not a single plastic-encased crayon. I sip my latte, reach for my muffin—and there is a small hand clutching the edge of my tabletop. The small hand belongs to a small child, maybe two years of age, who is happily toddling through the restaurant while his parent enjoys a few minutes of peace. The child beams and drools at me, resting his second hand on my table and making a noise of greeting that snags his parent's attention.

"Oh." She smiles, looking up and catching my eye. "He likes you."

Well, of course he likes me. I'm adorable. And he's reasonably cute himself, drool notwithstanding, so I'm glad to grin back and ruffle his curls. But then I'm done—ready to take out my awesome tablet and catch up on pressing news of the day, or possibly read the

Sweet Valley Confidential e-book that has somehow found its way to my Kindle—but what is this? My new little companion is not actually making his way back to Mom. He is continuing to emit happy grunting sounds, apparently believing he has found a kindred spirit here at the café, and now he is—ack! stop it!—grabbing at my iPad Air.

Have no fear; if I didn't put down this iPad to watch my kid's ballet class perform "Little Miss Muffet" at the spring recital, I'm certainly not going to let this kid take it away from me. (Just kidding! She was awesome, I'll send you the video on Facebook.) But I must admit that his determined hands and the rapidly rising intensity of his previously happy noises are kind of detracting from my enjoyment of this outing. So I look to his mother for help—but of course, she has no interest in calling her kid back. She's probably reading her own download of *Sweet Valley Confidential*, quite content to have turned her kid over to me.

People, this is completely unfair. I have a decent-sized heart. I genuinely like children (well, most of them). I am delighted to smile and blow a few kisses at your kid. Really, I am. But I am not here to babysit him while you take a break—and pretty much everyone else in the world feels the same way.

Believe me, I understand how you feel. You have already logged a million hours with your kid today, and as soon as you leave the café/store/park, you'll be logging a million more. The temptation to plop down on a bench and text long-lost friends while your kid shows the nice lady his entire fleet of new trucks is overwhelming. Surely the nice lady will enjoy interacting with your little cutie-pie . . . it's win-win, right?

Well, not so much. After a couple of trucks, I'm about done—because I'm not so into trucks, because I'm not so into your kid, but most of all because I've already been there, done that.

Here's the thing: Little kids need a lot of attention, but that doesn't last forever. At some point in the not-too-distant future, your kid will be in school and you will be having a child-free latte with a friend, and someone else's kid will be pawing your tabletop and trying to grab your awesome tablet, and you will wrinkle your nose in annoyance. Really, you will! You will wish that other parent would manage their own offspring, you will wonder why that other parent doesn't have an activity bag stuffed with items to Keep One Occupied (if you prefer not to lull your kid into a stupor by letting him play some idiotic game on your phone, try board books, finger puppets, Bendaroos, Color Wonder markers, and lacing cards), and you will smugly if not altogether accurately recollect how much better you were at handling these sorts of situations before your kid got too big to be exhilarated at the prospect of going to a restaurant with his mom rather than with his degenerate classmates who use the word "crap," like, all the time.

Certainly your kid is precious, and certainly he deserves and needs to experience positive attention from adults besides you, his devoted parent, which is why you should not keep him at home in a crate. But these facts are not license to turn him loose in public places and count on him to captivate complete strangers while you grab a half hour for yourself. While you may be thrilled to see young Xander "socializing" and "making friends," chances are great that after a couple of minutes, some admiring coos, and a quick round of peekaboo, his new acquaintances are ready to wave bye-bye and, by the way, would not mind a spritz of Purell to clean up the wet handprint their young buddy has left behind.

Lest you think I am concerned only with the lives of latte-sipping, truck-averse adults, let me provide you with a glimpse into the future, hopefully one whose truth you will in time realize only by observing your friends' annoying kids rather than trying to reprogram your own: An otherwise-appealing toddler who is allowed to roam free at restaurants, disturb other people, and demand attention from already-occupied grown-ups will eventually morph into a completely unappealing elementary schooler who interrupts adult conversations, refuses to sit quietly through proceedings not of engrossing interest to him (see the aforementioned performance of "Little Miss Muffet"), and behaves as if he is still the adorable center of the universe that his now-remorseful parents once imagined. It is much easier to rein in your kid now than it will be to deal with the consequences of not doing so later; and while these efforts may cost you a bit of me-time today, they will pay off beautifully when your seven-year-old is not the one jamming himself into the buffet line ahead of great-aunt Carol and helping himself to various appetizers with his fingers. Your future self will thank you—as will your future kid, who deep down would rather have the affection and goodwill of others than a handful of canapés.

And in the meantime, please do not feel condemned to Chuck E. Cheese's, or compelled to stockpile items to amuse your kid every time you venture into the adult world. If for some reason you are unable to avail yourself of the miracle of babysitters (yes, they're expensive, but if you and some friends take turns watching each other's kids, you will save major funds and also deepen your relationships—unless one of the kids routinely shows up with mucus streaming from his nose, which is totally a deal breaker), consider packing up an adult-type lunch (coffee, croissants, fruit, cheese, yum) and eating it with a pal at a park while your kids run around; inviting childless friends over for drinks or dessert at your home after your kid is in bed; finding one of those amazing places that offer a nice atmosphere for grown-ups as well as separate play areas for kids; or—if your kid just can't sit still, and you genuinely can't enjoy an outing without him taped to your side—limiting your excursions to more adult spots until he's older. Don't freak; it won't be as long as you think.

A quick note to those whose kids are not merely ambling about but are actually running around, screaming, and occasionally bumping into walls and other human beings: Do you remember how such shenanigans used to disgust you before you became a parent? Now, of course those thuggish hellions of old were an entirely different species than your darling Maverick, who "just needs to let off a little steam," but it's very difficult to tell the difference as he collides with my legs at eighty miles an hour. So if you could please corral your kid, that would be really outstanding. Thanks so much. And ow.

If you ever grow depressed that your child's presence has failed to enchant those around him, by the way, I suggest that you dress him up in something snappy and take him to a local nursing home. If he is old enough to sing a song or do the hand motions for "Itsy Bitsy Spider," this is icing on the cake; but even if he just sleeps in his stroller or hides his face in your shoulder while the residents beam at him, you will have done a really good thing. The joy his presence will elicit is truly beautiful; you will feel confirmed in your belief that your kid is the most wonderful creature on the planet, and I will get back to my latte.

YOUR KID WON'T SHARE

◆ ◆ ◆ ◆ ◆ ◆ ◆ ◆

I am telling you, getting Congress to work together is a fucking walk in the park compared to getting young Harry (not his real name, or is it?) to hand over the shape sorter to my kid in playgroup. You would figure this piece of molded plastic was Harry's mom the way he clung to it and the way he screamed and hit anytime my kid tried to get near the thing. Now, I am all for keeping the peace, and I honestly sort of enjoyed watching Harry carry on and thinking smugly to myself how much better behaved my own offspring was, but at some point it would have been nice for my kid to have the chance to sort a few shapes.

Harry's mom did not share her son's infatuation with the shape sorter; and after twenty or so minutes had elapsed, she began to wonder aloud if it was perhaps time for young Harry to yield the toy to another deserving child. She suggested this to Harry in a gentle, curious voice: "Sweetie, don't you want to give that little boy a turn with the shape sorter?" Harry did not. He did not actually use words to this effect; but as a perceptive observer of human behavior, I could surmise his reluctance from the angry "unnnnnh" he uttered as he clutched the toy more tightly. Harry's mom was stymied for a moment, then parleyed: "Maybe he could just hold one of the shapes?" This possibility also proved less than tantalizing to Harry, who grabbed all three shapes and sat on them. At that point I was not at all sure I wanted my own delicate child going near the shapes before they'd had a long bath in Purell, but Harry's mom was on a roll. "Sweetie, that's not nice. Please give that little boy one of the shapes." The shapes stayed where they were, and she gave me an apologetic look. "Harry's having such a hard time learning to share."

As I watched my own kid—cruelly denied the opportunity to develop his mastery of spatial relations but bravely amusing himself by chewing on a stuffed Elmo—I nodded at Harry's mom and allowed that, yeah, that did seem to be a growth edge for her kid. And that was pretty much the end of the conversation, as well as young Harry's foray into the world of sharing.

Here is some news, people: Your kid does not want to share. If you don't believe me, just ask him—"Sweetie, do you want to share?"—and witness his decidedly unenthusiastic response. Even at his tender age, he knows what the word means, and he hates it already.

I realize this may come as a shock, as you see your kid as sweet and generous and benevolent in every way—but please try to absorb it and move on. Your kid's hostility toward sharing does not preclude him from growing up into an Eastern mystic who renounces all physical possessions and lives a life of altruism and unselfishness, not that that is a career choice you are hoping he'll make. Your kid's refusing to share is actually perfectly normal—developmentally speaking, he's pretty much focused on himself and his own wants and needs; so, for all his brilliance, he may yet be incapable of comprehending why he should hand that shape sorter over to another kid, even one as adorable as my own.

Understanding your kid's reluctance to share, however, does not equate to enabling it.

There is a common fallacy among many parents that because a kid does not want to do something, he should not be required to do it. This belief has allowed thousands of young children to pass through toddlerhood without eating a single vegetable, as parents wait for their milk-shake-swilling offspring to evince an affinity for beets and kale, and to reach prekindergarten without sleeping through the night, as parents accustom themselves to small midnight visitors and breathlessly anticipate the day their children will stay in their awesomely tricked-out big-boy beds until dawn. This belief may also lead you to assume that your kid can hang on to a toy for as long as he damn well pleases—and that he doesn't have to relinquish it unless and until he's good and ready.

Hmmm. The rest of your playgroup—and the rest of the world—are not so convinced that this is the way to go. There are many other young children in the world, after all, some of whom would like to use the toys your kid is currently sitting on; and while these children may not interest you as much as your own child does, they do still deserve a modicum of consideration.

Here is some more news for you: Your kid is not unique. No kid likes to share. In fact, no adult really likes to share, either. Perhaps

I do not speak only for myself in confessing that when we are meeting for coffee and I order a lemon-poppy muffin—my absolute favorite, and the only muffin I have allowed myself to indulge in for, like, two months—and you ask me for a piece, my carefree smile and easygoing "Of course! Take as much as you want!" are totally, totally fake. However, share people do, even though we don't want to. Why? Because most people recognize that sharing is just part of the social contract, part of interacting with other human beings, annoying as they may be; whether we want to or not, we accept sharing as a responsibility of living in this world.

Of course your kid won't understand this, nor should you try to explain it all to him. But you do need to set your kid on the right path by demonstrating that people take turns and that—even if he does not want to—sharing is just one of those things he's going to need to do.

How can this be accomplished? While I actually really like Harry's mom, I have to say basically by doing the opposite of how she handled ShapeSorterGate. When you notice that your kid's been hogging a toy, or even that another kid is eyeing something your kid has had a decent amount of time with, briefly describe the situation to your kid: "You've had a good turn playing with the dump truck. You can play with it for another minute, and then it will be time to share with Noah." This tactic prepares your kid for the transition to come, acknowledging the fun that he's been having while warning him that change is on the way. If your kid protests, pay no attention—you are stating an incontrovertible fact, not asking his permission or opening a negotiation. When the minute is up, say calmly, "Now it's time to give Noah a turn with the dump truck."

Here's where the process breaks down for most parents. Their kid grabs the dump truck more tightly, or starts whining or crying or hollering or whatever, and the parent gets distracted from the task at hand. Endless rounds of "Okay, sweetie, one more minute," and "Please, honey, let Noah have the truck," and "You need to share with your friend" commence; and as they do, Noah sits sadly by, bereft of the promised dump truck, and the kid manages to evade the parent's well-intentioned but ultimately pointless and failed lesson on sharing.

But this need not happen to you! No matter how unpleasant your kid's reaction, you can simply forge ahead. How? Here's a trick that is so basic I have no idea why no one else seems to have come up with it: If your kid refuses to hand the dump truck over to Noah, take it away from your kid and hand it to Noah yourself. Problem solved! Noah is happy, and your kid—well, he's not happy, but he has learned that his parent means what she says and is not the bumbling pushover she perhaps appeared to be, and that ain't so bad. If your kid freaks out, remain calm; you can try to defuse the situation by distracting him with another toy (good luck!), acknowledging his feelings by saying something like, "I hear you're upset about sharing the truck. It can be hard to take turns, but sharing is the right thing to do," and praising him when he calms down—but don't belabor the point. He doesn't need you to lecture him on the importance of sharing, to offer a million hugs to mitigate the trauma of taking turns, or to beam "I'm so proud of you!" in a way that's more befitting a child who has just composed a sonata rather than a child who has just cried his eyes out over handing off a toy to a pal. Rather, your kid needs you to stay steady and matter-of-fact—and yes, he may also need you to remove him from playgroup long enough to get himself together and stop lunging at Noah with bared teeth.

Over time your kid will grow resigned to sharing—we all do!—but it will be a smoother path if you can provide some happy associations with sharing as well. Be sure to use the word "share" whenever positive and appropriate; pointing out that a pal is "sharing" with your kid by giving him a turn with a toy or that you are "sharing" with your kid by giving him a bite of your lemon-poppy muffin (grrrr) will help him understand that he, too, is a beneficiary of this practice. You can also teach him that sharing is not an all-the-time obligation; when hosting playgroup or even just a playdate, you can explain that everyone has a few (emphasize "few," so his entire toy collection isn't declared off-limits) special possessions that can be hidden away rather than shared with guests.

But in your quest to make sharing palatable to your kid, don't widen your eyes, smile brightly, and tell him how fun it is to share with his friends. It's not really fun—it's actually hard and kind of sucky—and your kid will see right through you and your false cheer. It's also fine for your kid to do stuff that's hard and kind of sucky—but that, like sharing, is still nice, and fair, and good, and all those other commendable qualities that you hope your kid will acquire but which he can't possibly develop unless he lets someone else have a turn with Elmo already. I mean, really.

YOUR KID IS TAKING OVER THE HOUSE

◆ ◆ ◆ ◆ ◆ ◆ ◆ ◆

Remember how exciting it was to decorate your home? Painting the walls, picking out rugs, investing in a few nice pieces of furniture, finding a place for that revolting vase sufficiently out of the way that you wouldn't have to look at it every day but not so far out of the way that your mother-in-law could scold you for failing to display it? Good times.

Things may be looking a bit, er, different around the house today. I know how you feel: On the eve of the birth of my first kid, my husband and I had a gorgeous dining room set—dark wooden table, granite-topped serving buffet, and more chairs than we could possibly need. Even though we used it maybe four times a year, we absolutely loved the set and how grown-up it made us feel. Honestly, the thing was awesome.

Less than twelve months after our kid was born, the thing was also wrapped in plastic and consigned to the farthest reaches of our garage. In its place were the same decorative touches that probably brighten your domicile today: a play kitchen with faux-stainless appliances nicer than our real ones, a kiddie-sized table and chairs festooned with bits of dried playdough and an almost-empty juice box, and a mini basketball hoop whose ball would go missing about eighty times a day. Also Sesame Street train cars on the windowsill.

I am not saying that the conversion of our once-amazing formal dining room into a playroom was a terrible thing. Like yours, our kid needed space to explore and frolic and discover and all that. Like you, my husband and I savored the certainty that we were being good parents, the kind who cheerfully sacrifice the trappings of prechild life in order to provide the best possible environment for their kid. And honestly, we needed a place to store the millions of toys and art supplies and accessories and shit we'd been so eager to amass, much more than we needed a dining room set we could not imagine Ever. Using. Again.

So yeah, you've made absolutely the right decision in letting your kid—and your kid's stuff—take over your home. Except that—well, don't you sometimes wish you had your house back?

I did not unwrap my dining room table for close to six years (sniff). But people, please learn from my mistakes! Don't wait that long to reclaim at least some of the accouterments of your prechild life. Yes, your kid is entitled to feel that your casa is su casa, and yes, you will have to compromise your design aesthetic to accommodate her need to explore and frolic and discover and all that. But these considerations do not extend to every room, every wall, and every surface—and neither do they mean your kid should be making such an enormous mess of your home.

I know this sounds kid unfriendly and sort of mean, but I promise it's not. Actually, bringing back some of your adult furniture—and relegating some of your kid's effects to the attic, garage, or basement—is an excellent move for both you and your kid. For one thing, your kid is probably overwhelmed by the sheer amount of stuff she has. If she's got a pretend kitchen, a pretend grocery store, and a pretend woodworking shop all within a ten-foot radius of one another, chances are not great that she's able to focus and really engage with any of them on a regular basis. And while she may still be too young to truly take pride in her belongings, she'll have a much easier time learning to treat her toys properly if she doesn't have an endless supply scattered on the floor of every room.

Reclaiming some adult areas is also a fantastic way to introduce your kid to the concept of personal space. For example: If your bedroom is home not only to your bed, clothing, and dresser but also to a large stuffed bear and an adorable wicker box filled with board books and the stray Fisher-Price Little Person, you are essentially sharing a room with your kid. Now, I realize your kid is delightful company, possibly better than your grumpy spouse who never cleans out the shower drain and refuses to accompany you to salsa dancing lessons even though Melissa's husband takes her every week, but this is really not the best dynamic to establish. Your kid should feel welcome in your room, of course, but she should also recognize that it is your room—not just another space for her to enter and plunder at will. Guiding your kid to knock before entering your bedroom, to take her things with her when she leaves, and to ask permission before handling your stuff or jumping on your bed are easy ways to communicate that this space belongs to you;

and learning this lesson will help your kid begin to understand the importance of personal space—and of treating other people's space, and the things in it, with respect and courtesy.

And this lesson should extend past the door of your bedroom. Refusing to allow your active kid to climb on the kitchen counter; declining to take an appealingly colorful but extremely fragile ceramic figurine down from the mantel so your kid can "play" with it, even though you're pretty sure she's a tactile learner and you want to nurture an interest in sculpture; restricting her use of glitter glue to the backyard or maybe the breakfast table (not the couch—you would not think I'd need to say this, but you'd be surprised); and closing off certain areas of the house not only to ensure the safety of your kid, but also to ensure the safety of the prized possessions inside, are everyday, matter-of-fact practices that will teach your kid about boundaries and limits. And the earlier you can get your kid recognizing and respecting boundaries and limits—oh my gosh, the easier and more pleasant your life will be.

It's not only the rooms and the stuff that matter, of course—it's what the rooms and the stuff symbolize. Again, remember setting up your first home? Whether it was a six-bedroom mansion in the best school district (I'm jealous!) or a cramped single in the worst dorm with a shared bathroom down the hall (I'm with you!), you arranged the home in a way that reflected you—your personality, your interests, your values. These don't disappear when you have a kid—and though you may not realize it until your kid gets a little older and you get a little more of your old self back, neither does the need to honor and express them. Shoving aside your favorite furniture, your cherished tchotchkes, your preference for clean lines or shabby elegance or artfully arranged clutter so that your kid's stuff can spread out to every room in the house—well, that's just not fair.

And no, wanting your house to go back a little more to the way it used to be is not selfish. While the toy industry may preach differently, please be assured that giving your kid affection and warmth and love, and instilling in her confidence and happiness and security, have nothing to do with the amount of square footage devoted to her paraphernalia. A kid whose toys take up every room in the house but whose resentful parent dreams of the day she can get rid of them all is in a much worse place than a kid whose toys are confined to one or two rooms but whose parent genuinely enjoys joining her for a session of play. I mean, really.

Even with these restrictions, of course, your home probably holds plenty of space for your kid to play—and plenty of things for her to play with. And a significant part of that play is going to make a total mess. That is great, actually—your kid's developing gross motor skills, blossoming creativity, and just general age and stage call for big, jumbled, chaotic playtimes; and if you are willing to go with the flow, you'll actually find them quite adorable and charming. Please don't hesitate to get on the floor with your kid and join in the fun; stamp pad art is every bit as fabulous as you remember, as are diving into a huge box of cast-off clothes for dress-up, growling "vroom" and rolling fleets of toy cars all over the carpet, and building a block city that takes up the entire den.

But just as it's good for you to join your kid in making these messes, it's also good for her to join you in cleaning them up. Feel free to make cleanup as enjoyable as possible—sing that cleanup song that seems to lodge in your head the moment you become a parent, challenge your kid to a cleanup race, or work as a team to restore some semblance of order to the room—but be sure that she gets the job done. Don't let her scamper off to another activity while you sort blocks and console yourself that at least she's having fun; remember that the point of this exercise is not for your kid to extend her happy play experience but to learn the values of responsibility and orderliness.

Hopefully all this cleaning will yield not only a tidier home but also a sleepier child—one who will eagerly climb in bed for a nap while you, my friend, enjoy a delicious snack at your very own dining room table.

SECTION 2

Your Bratty Child—Ages Five Through Ten

INTRODUCING YOUR BRATTY CHILD

◆ ◆ ◆ ◆ ◆ ◆ ◆ ◆

Congratulations! You have seriously accomplished something amazing. The little blob—the most precious little blob in the universe, yes, but a little blob nonetheless—who needed you every single second for every single thing has grown up. Not that he's entirely ready to launch—but he is ready to get himself dressed, poop in the potty, walk without clutching your outstretched hands, draw a picture without eating the crayon, and generally make it through the day without your constant and unyielding attention. And that, my friend, is nothing to sneeze at.

However, as you may suspect, your job is not quite over. In addition to chauffeuring your kid around and preparing his meals and buying him shit, you are also charged with instilling in him some common decency. Examples include not interrupting people all the time, saying please and thank you rather than grabbing and running off, speaking politely, conducting himself with a modicum of dignity at dinnertime—a whole gigantic list of skills your kid exhibits no interest whatsoever in adopting.

And skills that you may argue your kid doesn't even need—at least, not right now. He's great exactly the way he is, smart-ass remarks (so precocious!) and sobbing every time he loses a game (and sensitive!) and all. Your top priority isn't turning your, uh, feisty kid into some please-and-thank-you automaton, crushing his creative spirit by placing a whole lot of annoying demands upon him, or implying that his real and authentic self is lacking in any way. Your top priorities are nurturing your kid's unique spark, giving him the encouragement he needs in order to grow and thrive, and inspiring him to love himself and to feel he has an honored place in the world. Because, you know, that's what good parents do.

It may surprise you that I am actually in favor of all these things. Unique sparks, growing and thriving, inspiration and honored places, even, uh, feistiness—yes, yes, yes, and yes! But I remain firmly convinced that your kid can enjoy all these gifts without becoming a total undisciplined brat. And that making this happen is what good parents do.

A big part of your kid's job during these years is figuring out how he fits in. As a baby, and maybe even as a toddler and preschooler, he was taught that he's the center of everything—that attention and resources and focus belong to him and him alone. But that attitude just can't be sustained any longer. Of course he's important, and of course he's special, but it's time for him to learn that he's one of many important and special people who also deserve attention and resources and focus. If he fails to master this lesson, he'll devolve into a spoiled, self-centered kid who has trouble getting along with just about anyone not consumed entirely with meeting his needs and wants. But if he does master this lesson, he'll understand how to treat people, how to empathize and cooperate and bond, and how to get his needs and wants met without alienating or hurting others. And the positive feedback, the friendships, and the generally pleasant interactions he'll have with those around him—including you!—will ultimately help him grow into the happy, confident, wonderful person both you and he want him to be.

Believe it or not, your kid will achieve these lofty goals by starting small—by adopting the aforementioned skills of not interrupting, saying please and thank you, etc. Simple as they may seem, these behaviors teach your kid a great deal: that people besides himself are entitled to respect, how to demonstrate courtesy for adults, how to enjoy himself while still observing some basic social conventions. And you can talk until you're blue in the face (but please don't) about how important it is to treat others with kindness—but if between these high-minded speeches, you're letting your kid lie and mouth off and ruin meals with his horrific table manners, your words won't mean a thing.

Just one small note before you read on: You may notice that there's a bit of age overlap between this section and the next. That's because—lucky you!—your bratty child may already be evincing some behaviors associated with bratty tweens, and another equally lucky parent may have a tween who's still wallowing in bratty child habits. So feel free to read ahead or to come back here as needed. You're always welcome!

Okay, ready to get started? This section will explain it all. I almost promise.

YOUR KID INTERRUPTS

◆ ◆ ◆ ◆ ◆ ◆ ◆ ◆

I'm not convinced I'm the most fascinating person in the world, but I am convinced of this: Whatever I'm saying to you on the phone is infinitely more interesting than whatever your kid is hollering in the background. So why are you paying so much attention to her?

I understand emergencies come up; and believe me, if your kid needs you to fish her out of the toilet or something, I will graciously end the call. But if your kid has just decided that she'd like more blue corn tortilla chips, wants to show you a Lego contraption she's spent all of eight minutes constructing, or has a question about elephants, may I suggest you withhold your immediate and undivided attention until you and I have finished discussing the economies of emerging Latin American markets or some equally worthy topic such as Brangelina? May I suggest you give her a sunny smile while shaking your head and pointing to the telephone? Very rapidly she will learn what this means—and better yet, she will learn not to interrupt.

We spend so much time hanging on our children's every word that we can't really blame them for assuming we don't want to miss a single syllable—even if we already happen to be engaged with another reasonably diverting human being. But there are occasions—many of them—that our kids need to pipe down and wait their turn; and if you can't focus on a fifteen- or even ten-minute conversation without your kid interrupting, it's probably time to teach her that skill.

Now, the image of an adult blathering away to a friend while her child stands forlorn, stymied in her attempt to communicate some deep and significant truth, is a horrible one, and I am not urging you to model yourself after those awful parents who collect their kids from school and hustle them into the car without once looking up from their phones. (Really, people, you can't take five seconds to greet your Willow? Are you guiding a drone or something?) But surely there is a vast gulf between displaying such complete disregard for the person you have brought into the world and cheerfully telling the other participants in a midday conference call that you will have to put them on hold because your kid has just informed you that her arm hurts. So before implementing any anti-interruption techniques, engage in a quick self-assessment to be sure that your kid does enjoy periods of your undivided attention, that you take the time to look her in the eye and listen to what she's saying, that you encourage her to share and communicate—check, check, check? Good. Then we're ready to go.

First, accept the reality that you are indeed about to dislodge your child from the constant and primary center of your attention—and that this is actually a good thing. If she is accustomed to claiming your focus anytime, anyplace, this of course will be a big change for her, but not one that needs to be some big traumatic deal. Your kid waits her turn to speak at school, presumably, and doesn't go around interrupting her teachers and classmates all the time, but she still feels like a valued student and friend, right? As long as you are calm and positive about setting similar expectations, she will remain every bit as confident and attached as she was before—as well as a lot more socially adept and pleasant to be around.

Choose a neutral time just before you plan to implement your new method, and explain that you are about to make an important call/have friends over/visit with a pal/whatever and that you will need to give it/them your full attention. Let your kid know that if she has an emergency—you may need to define this as bleeding or vomiting to clarify that a sudden desire for juice doesn't qualify—she should get you but that otherwise she will need to amuse herself for a while. If she has not yet learned to amuse herself (in which case you most definitely need the rest of this book), you can help her prepare a selection of toys, art supplies, or snacks, or set a timer so she can visualize how much longer she will be on her own. You can even set up a small cardboard container labeled "Message Box" that she can fill with thoughts and news for you to read once you've finished your visit or call. Not only will writing and decorating these messages keep her busy and engaged, but they are also super-cute snapshots of what your kid was feeling and experiencing on a particular day or at a particular age. Samples from my personal Message Box: "I don't have any clean skorts. Oh, I found one," and "There is a cockroach in my room." Really, these are keepers!

When you are in a longer or larger gathering with your kid—a family party, maybe, or another intergenerational-type event—your kid will have an opportunity to learn nonverbal social cues, or how to break into a conversation graciously. Teach your kid to approach quietly and stand nearby when you are chatting with a group of adults and she wants your attention, and be sure to reward her by turning to her as soon as you politely can with a big smile. Although signals like touching a parent's elbow or hand are also popular ways for a kid to convey she needs you, don't use them exclusively—they can be effective, but they're not always applicable in the wider world.

Of course, the road to noninterruption is paved with plenty of interruption. However, you will smooth the road by reinforcing for your kid that interrupting is not a worthwhile path. Once your kid understands the rules, feel free to take your phone call in another room and close the door behind you if she continues to interrupt; to drive the point home, you might also adopt a policy that the answer to any request posed via interruption will be a nonnegotiable no.

And last of all, let's reconsider the most common response to an interrupting kid: Shifting your attention from the person you're talking to—perhaps me, for instance, a person with a life and obligations of her own who's still managed to cobble together time for a grown-up chat with you—and giving your interrupting kid a lecture on not interrupting. People, this never succeeds. Why? First of all, your kid is going to hear virtually nothing you are saying because lectures don't work (skip ahead to the next chapter if you don't believe me), and second of all, you have just rewarded your kid's interrupting! While she may be interrupting in hopes of obtaining a cookie or your resolution (in her favor) of an argument with her sibling on a compelling topic like TV or I-had-that-first, your attention is an excellent consolation prize. As you are winding up your treatise on Rudeness and Respect for Mommy's Time, while incidentally I am still hanging on the phone, though I must admit I have begun thumbing through a magazine, your kid will be absorbing only the fact that interrupting works—and gleefully adding this tactic to her arsenal for future use.

YOUR KID DOESN'T LISTEN THE FIRST TIME

◆ ◆ ◆ ◆ ◆ ◆ ◆ ◆

Let me know which of these scenarios sounds most familiar (they are fun to do as dialogues, especially with a shy person who speaks only in monosyllables!):

> YOU, 5:00 p.m.: Sweetie, your clean laundry's on your bed. Please put it away before baseball, okay?
>
> KID: Uh-huh.
>
> YOU, 5:15 p.m.: Sweetie, it's almost time to leave for baseball. Did you put your laundry away?
>
> KID: Uh-uh. But I will.
>
> YOU (chipper): Great!
>
> YOU, 5:30 p.m.: Sweetie, it's time to leave for baseball. Did you put your laundry away?
>
> KID: Uh-uh. But I will.
>
> YOU: I guess you can do it when we get home.

YOU, 8:15 p.m.: Sweetie, it's time to get in bed. Please put your laundry away first so it doesn't end up all over the floor.

KID: 'Kay.

YOU, 8:30 p.m.: Sweetie, your laundry is all over the floor. Why didn't you put it away?

KID: I'm too tired.

Here's another:

YOU, 6:00 p.m.: Sweetie, it'll be time for dinner in half an hour. Please finish up your homework!

KID: It's done.

YOU (chipper): Great! You can play on the computer before dinner if you want.

KID: 'Kay.

YOU, 6:20 p.m.: Sweetie, dinner is almost ready. Please finish your game and get washed up.

KID: 'Kay.

YOU, 6:25 p.m.: Sweetie, are you still on the computer?

KID: Uh-huh.

YOU: Sweetie, I told you to finish your game! Please close it down and get washed up.

KID: 'Kay.

YOU, 6:33 p.m.: Sweetie, dinner is on the table! Are you still on the computer?

KID: Uh-huh.

YOU: Sweetie, I told you to finish your game! Please close it down and get washed up right now.

KID: 'Kay.

Aren't these entertaining? Here's one more:

YOU, 8:00 p.m.: Sweetie, it's almost time to get in bed. Please get your backpack all packed up for school tomorrow.

KID: I did.

YOU: You're sure? You put your math book inside and everything?

KID: Uh-huh.

YOU (chipper): Great!

YOU, 8:20 p.m.: Sweetie, is this your math book on the couch?

KID: What? Oh. Yeah.

YOU: I thought you said it was in your backpack.

KID: I thought it was.

YOU: Well, it's not. Please pack it up before you get in bed, okay?

KID: 'Kay.

YOU, 7:30 a.m. the next day: Sweetie, is this your math book still on the couch?

KID: What? Oh. Yeah.

YOU: I thought you put it in your backpack last night!

KID: Uh-uh.

YOU: Well, please do it now, okay?

KID: 'Kay.

YOU, 7:40 a.m.: Sweetie, it's time to leave for school. Please grab your backpack, and be sure your math book is inside, okay?

KID: It's not in there.

YOU: Well, where is it?

KID: I'm not sure. I think it's on the couch.

As ridiculous as these exchanges sound in real time, they look even more insane written out, don't they? And they raise the suspicion that your kid has a pretty significant problem. Are there hearing issues? It seems that way—except that he can hear you talking about his less-than-stellar social studies test or the possibility of his getting a new bike from, like, four rooms away. So maybe he has difficulty concentrating? That must be it—except that he can focus intently on his computer game or practicing pitches for over an hour at a time. So . . . what is it? Seriously, what the fuck is wrong with your kid?

Let's do a little investigative work and look for clues in how these exchanges end:

Exchange #1

YOU, 8:30 p.m.: Sweetie, your laundry is all over the floor. Why didn't you put it away?

KID: I'm too tired.

YOU: I know, it's been a long day. And you're always so sleepy after baseball! Here, I'll put your laundry away tonight. You can do it next time, okay?

KID: Zzzz.

Exchange #2

YOU, 6:33 p.m.: Sweetie, dinner is on the table! Are you still on the computer?

KID: Uh-huh.

YOU: Sweetie, I told you to finish your game! Please close it down and get washed up right now.

KID: 'Kay.

YOU: And please hurry! We're all waiting for you.

KID: I said 'kay!

Exchange #3

YOU, 7:40 a.m.: Sweetie, it's time to leave for school. Please grab your backpack, and be sure your math book is inside, okay?

KID: It's not in there.

YOU: Well, where is it?

KID: I'm not sure. I think it's on the couch.

YOU: Yes, it's still there! I'll grab it for you. But please be more responsible next time, okay?

KID: 'Kay.

Now we are getting somewhere! It's pretty clear that there is no problem at all. You tell your kid to do something; he ignores you. You tell him to do something again; he ignores you again. Eventually, you give up and take care of everything for him. This is actually the opposite of a problem. This is fantastic!

Well, it's fantastic for your kid in the short term, anyway. But this book is not really about making things fantastic for your kid in the short term—and if you're reading it, you've probably moved beyond that goal as well. We're here for your long-term kid, and, by the way, for you, too. And the status quo is pretty lousy for both.

I realize that in the moment, it's so much easier to take care of things yourself than to continue badgering your less-than-responsive kid. But the choice is not actually between those two options; it's between getting your kid to listen to you or not. And although your current course of action is heavy on the "or not," it's not too late to make a change.

So what are we going to do instead? Let's consider the possibilities:

POSSIBILITY #1: Yell. This is a pretty popular response, and rather cathartic in the short term. But remember: We're all about the long term here. And while yelling may galvanize your kid to do as he's told a couple of times, it loses its power rapidly. Yelling also teaches your kid that he doesn't need to listen to you until you raise your voice. Plus, it makes you look sort of desperate and out of control. Plus, it damages your relationship. So, no.

POSSIBILITY #2: Nag. Everyone hates this one. It's no fun to be the nagger, the naggee, or the bystander listening to said nagging. Plus it doesn't work. If it did, your kid would be sitting at the dinner table with his hands washed—but you and I both know he's still on the computer. So, no.

POSSIBILITY #3: Quietly but firmly, tell your kid to do something exactly once—and back up your words with calm, effective action. This response gives you an aura of authority, a respite from yelling and nagging, and a break from picking up your kid's laundry every time he's tired, which is, like, always. It's a winner!

This last one is easy to implement, too. Basically, you do exactly what you're doing—except you stop after your first line. "Please put your clean laundry away." Done! "Please wash up for dinner." Done! "Please pack up your backpack before bed." Done!

Now, I realize your kid won't hop to the first—and now only—time he hears you. After all, why should he? He's been trained to put you off until the task is convenient for him, or until you take care of it yourself. But that phenomenon is about to end—and when it does, his response time will improve dramatically.

He may not care when his neatly folded laundry ends up all over the floor because he couldn't be bothered to put it away—until he needs a clean shirt three days later and finds it crumpled under the bed. He may not care that his extended screen time is cutting into the dinner hour—until he emerges from the computer room to find that his food is cold and, by the way, he doesn't have enough time to eat dessert before bed. And he may not care that his detested textbook has escaped from his backpack—until his teacher makes him stay in for recess as a punishment for coming unprepared to class.

What's so great about this course of action is that your kid experiences logical consequences for failing to listen to you—and that you have absolutely nothing to do with meting them out. While yelling, nagging, and taking over his chores damage your relationship and his developing autonomy, simply sitting back and letting real life wash over your kid is as easy as it is effective. And it won't be long before your kid not only realizes you mean business and starts heeding you—but also begins to internalize certain habits and responsibilities.

While your kid is experiencing this learning curve—and enduring the difficulties and setbacks that accompany not-listening-the-first-time—remember to remain consistent, calm, and loving. It's tempting to follow up your matter-of-fact "I guess you'll need to wear a different shirt" or "Hopefully you'll have time for dessert tomorrow night" with a twist-of-the-knife remark like, "Maybe next time you'll listen to me" or "That's what happens when you don't do what I tell you"—but don't, don't, don't. Your kid is not a complete fool; he's already connected the dots and knows you're right, but he'll (rightfully) resent your rubbing it in. The point of this exercise is, after all, not to increase your kid's reliance on you but ultimately to increase his ability to rely on himself.

With all this listening suddenly going on, you also have a great opportunity to make sure it moves both ways. Not only should your kid listen to you—but you should listen to him as well. If all you're getting out of your kid's waking hours are monosyllables, maybe that's because all you're saying to him is "Do this" or "Have you done that?" or "It's time for [whatever]." I realize extracting meaningful conversation from your kid is like pulling teeth—but that doesn't excuse you from trying. Even if he seems totally unaware of the fact that you're taking the time to come into his room to speak with him rather than yelling from the hallway; totally uninterested in your effort to maintain eye contact rather than checking your phone when you think he's not looking; totally unseeing of the cheerful smile that rises to your lips when he enters a room; and totally unappreciative of the friendly-but-not-overbearing questions you're asking about his day and his opinions—well, he's actually very aware, very interested, very seeing, and very appreciative. More appreciative, even, than you would be if he would put his damn math book away already. And that's a lot.

YOUR KID NEEDS TO BUCK UP

◆ ◆ ◆ ◆ ◆ ◆ ◆ ◆

Did you know that when my kid went ice-skating for the first time, I made him wear a helmet? He was nine.

I am not bringing this up to raise awareness about the perils of ice-skating, nor to make you feel like a rank amateur when it comes to fearing the world and what it might do to your kid. I am actually pretty embarrassed about the episode—though probably not as embarrassed as my kid was tooling around the rink with a helmet on—and share it for only one reason: to prove to you that, yes, I get it.

I totally get that you want your kid to be safe and protected and comfortable. The universe is not always a fabulous place; unpleasant things happen, and of course you want to keep your kid helmeted, at least figuratively. It feels natural to pad the corners, cover the outlets, remove the obstacles, smooth the way. After all, isn't that what good parents do?

Well, yeah—up to a point. But once that point passes—and

considering that you're reading this section, it probably has—that kind of parenting actually starts to hurt your kid. If you're in the habit of checking out all the fun articles eager to explain how every single thing you're doing as a parent is totally wrong and stupid, surely you're already well acquainted with the avalanche of studies detailing why kids need to face difficulty, cope with challenge, and develop resilience—and how too much hovering, too much devotion, and too much smoothing impede that growth.

But even without reading those articles, don't you already sense that something has gone awry with your kid? As you're running to fetch a Band-Aid for your weeping eight-year-old's skinned elbow, meticulously cutting every bit of crust off your school-age kid's SunButter sandwich, or entering your third hour of commiserating about the unfairness of Mikayla's being awarded a solo at the guitar recital—even though your kid really, really (sob! hiccup), really wanted it—isn't a part of you wondering why your kid is making such a huge deal out of things? Isn't a part of you wishing that your kid would just buck up?

Because, yeah, she should. Right up there with cursive and penmanship, "bucking up" is one of the lost values of our time. And oh my gosh, I totally miss it.

What is "bucking up"? Basically, just what it sounds like. Bucking up is having something unpleasant happen but not freaking out; it's falling down and getting up; it's acknowledging disappointment and sadness without making the aforementioned huge deal out of things. Bucking up is not an instinct—in my experience, a far more instinctive response to the pitfalls of life is picking a fight with one's partner (sorry, honey!) or disappearing into one's room with a pint of gelato and a spoon—but it is a skill that your kid desperately needs.

First a disclaimer: Of course your kid has a right to her emotions. She should never feel compelled to shut anger and frustration inside or to pretend everything's fine when it's absolutely not. But that doesn't necessarily mean that she should be throwing fits when things don't go her way or reacting to a minor injury with a full-on set of histrionics, you know? And like so much else, her ability to tell the difference—and to react appropriately—begins with you.

This is especially tough because—those aforementioned articles notwithstanding—the kind of parenting we're encouraged to practice these days is not all that conducive to bucking up. Imagine your kid experiencing discomfort or pain—not rupturing-appendix-type pain, just taking a spill on her bike or coughing up some water that went down the wrong way. Then imagine doing absolutely nothing about it. Then imagine every other parent you know watching you do nothing.

It's a terrifying prospect, isn't it? Because you understand what's expected—the loud gasp, the rushing over to check out what went wrong, the cooing and soothing and wiping away tears. Doing anything less, and for sure doing nothing at all, seems like a hostile act—hostile not only to your kid but to the entire ethos of parenting.

But it's actually a pretty fantastic act. After all, you've got plenty of opportunities to show your kid you care about her—you don't need to engage in this big dramatic gesture to prove your love. And you've got plenty of opportunities to wow your fellow parents by showering your kid with copious amounts of adoration and affection in their presence. But what you may not have are plenty of opportunities to show your kid that you believe she's competent, that you expect her to handle minor adversity on her own, that you trust she'll come through fine—in short, that she needs to buck up. Don't miss this one, okay?

If your kid is accustomed to having you sprint to her side every time she suffers a setback, this will be quite a change for you both. Be sure she understands that your new reaction comes from a place of love and care, not hostility or disinterest; you don't want to shame or scold her for being upset—you just want to show that she can cope with whatever is happening to her. "Wow, that is a big scrape. I'm sorry you fell! Make sure you wash it off really well before you put on a Band-Aid—they're in the bathroom closet." "It's so disappointing that your painting didn't get displayed in the hallway. I know you worked hard on it. Maybe yours will be picked next semester." "I saw that kid run into you, and I bet it hurts. If you want to keep playing, though, it's time to get back in the game." Delivered in a calm, affectionate voice, phrases like these express sympathy for your kid's plight without making it a bigger deal than it needs to be; they also let her decide how she wants to handle the situation and encourage her to do so with positive, appropriate action. For example: Does she really want to stand there crying and bleeding, or should she maybe take care of the scrape before the blood drips on her cute new tennis shoes? Is throwing a world-class fit over being bumped worth missing out on playing the rest of the game? After a while, you may not even need to say a word; and the parents shooting you death looks when you fail to attend immediately to your kid's taking a tumble will start regarding you with respect (and envy) when she stands up and nonchalantly gets back to whatever she had been doing.

Please note, however, that bucking up does not begin the moment your kid experiences discomfort/rejection/disappointment and end the moment she bounces back. Bucking up really encompasses a much broader worldview; it's about keeping your situation in perspective and understanding that what happens to you is not necessarily the most important thing going on in the universe at that moment. Again, this is not a particularly popular message to give our kids today—but it's a good one, and one that will pay dividends not only when your kid loses a contest or falls down at the ice rink but also in your day-to-day life.

How does this work? It's pretty simple: Basically, you keep your kid in perspective—not your perspective, where of course she's the epicenter of everything, but the perspective of the wider world—and behave accordingly. This means that if you're getting on a train and there's just one empty seat, it doesn't automatically go to your kid. If you're visiting a friend and she offers your kid a glass of water, you don't explain that your kid really prefers organic milk or juice—real juice—not a juice drink that's, like, ninety-four percent high-fructose corn syrup—you just let your kid say "yes, please" or "no, thank you." If you're feeling totally snug in your house but your kid complains she's cold, you don't spring up to adjust the heater—you just tell her to get a sweater. You will be amazed to realize how often you put your kid's comfort and preferences ahead of your own, and even ahead of basic social niceties—and how much her bucking-up skills will improve once you knock it off.

Teaching your kid to buck up really brings an amazing cascade of benefits. As much as you might think your kid loves the attention you're giving to every instant of her life, and your abiding devotion to soothing her after every disappointment, she's old enough to sense that she should be handling some of this on her own—and to wonder if you're jumping in because she's just not competent. You actually help her more by backing off; in doing so, you allow her to develop self-reliance and resilience and you show that you trust her judgment and resourcefulness. You also keep your kid from embarrassing herself; trust me, plenty of people are watching your kid and thinking she's way too old to be carrying on like this. And finally, you make life significantly more pleasant not only for your kid but for everyone around her; having spent way too many hours attending to school-age children (not mine, are you kidding?) howling for literally twenty minutes over a bruised leg, locking themselves in my daughter's room during a playdate because the other girls "won't do the things I want to do!" and tearfully demanding to play inside after spotting a bee (no, the kid was not allergic) across the backyard, I can personally attest to the joy a few more bucked-up kids would bring to this world.

YOUR KID RUINS MEALS

◆ ◆ ◆ ◆ ◆ ◆ ◆ ◆

Pretty much every expert agrees: Shared meals are one of the best ways to build a strong, secure, and happy family.

Clearly these people have never been to dinner at your home.

Seriously, as if getting your kid fed and organized weren't hard enough, now you have the pressure of gathering everybody around the table, creating a joyful atmosphere, fostering meaningful conversation, and instilling a few manners to boot. No wonder you're throwing up your hands in despair at your parental inadequacies, or figuring these supposed experts don't know what the hell they're talking about and banishing them from your mind completely.

But maybe there's a middle ground here. (There is!) Maybe shared meals could be a bit more frequent, a bit more enjoyable, a bit more special—and maybe the key to all that is your kid.

Our kids' earliest years are so all-consuming that we sometimes don't realize they've grown older, more capable of self-control and mature behavior. And one of the last places our school-age kids get away with acting like, well, like babies is around the dinner table. It's time for that to change.

While your kid is still rightfully counting on you to shoulder responsibility for most of his meal-related needs, you can start giving him a few responsibilities as well. He's old enough to do more than show up, eat (or complain, then possibly eat), deploy whatever manners or conversational tidbits he feels like deploying, and scoot back to his video game as soon as he's swallowed his last bite. He's old enough to be a full participant in the meal—with the attitude, obligations, and privileges that the term implies.

Let's tackle the attitude first. The days of you setting the table, preparing the meal, and cleaning up while your kid lolls about should be o-v-e-r. Whether it's putting out plates and flatware (this is a great opportunity to teach your kid the proper way to set a table, by the way: knife edge facing the plate, drinking glass on the right—he can handle it); clearing the table and loading the dishwasher; rinsing fruit and veggies; or doing some mixing, measuring, pouring, and stirring, your kid should be in the kitchen and by your side. Not only is it nice to have an extra pair of hands around (especially after you've been doing this a couple of weeks, at which point the hands will be significantly more helpful), but it's also nice to teach your kid that meals don't magically appear on the table and that he has a role in making them happen. You'll also find that your kid is much less likely to reject a dish that he's taken part in preparing or to remain completely unaware of the presence of a fork (no, pasta is not a finger food, sweetie, not even those cute bow ties) if he's painstakingly placed one in the exact middle of every napkin on the table. The more invested your kid is in a meal, the better his attitude—and the better the entire family's experience—will be.

And once your kid is at the table—well, let's make sure he's enhancing the mealtime experience, okay? Because slouching over his plate, refusing to eat anything whose ingredients don't coincide exactly with his list of likes, holding up a drumstick and licking off the seasoning (gross but true story), and wiping his filthy mouth with his napkin (yay), then depositing said napkin next to your drinking glass (not so yay) is not really doing much for the atmosphere, as far as I can tell. Neither is his interrupting that fascinating story you were sharing to announce that he needs more water, getting up from the table at random, or contributing to the dinner conversation solely through burps and the occasional comment on his sister's stupidity.

Your kid is unlikely to alter these charming practices on his own—especially if your reaction is to sigh, scold, ignore, or yell rather than teach him a better way. But have no fear: This is the perfect time to mount a campaign to improve your kid's mealtime behavior. He's old enough to get it, he's young enough to master new habits, and he's still malleable enough to respond to simple and logical positive and negative consequences.

Begin in a positive, inclusive way; rather than announcing that he's old enough to shape up, damn it, tell your kid that you want to make mealtime more special for the entire family—and that that includes upgrading everybody's manners and behavior. If your kid has not received a primer on basic table manners, now is the time; make sure he knows to put his napkin in his lap, stay in his seat, sit up straight, use his silverware, eat over his plate, take reasonably sized bites, chew with his mouth closed—all the highlights. (If you're not convinced he's the right age to practice these manners, just imagine someone you like and respect suddenly appearing at the table and watching your kid eat—you get it now, right?) Similarly, your kid should be taught not to burp or fart at the table (I mean, really) and not to engage in what my family calls "mindless chatter"—an awesome term that covers everything from insulting one's siblings to reciting rap lyrics to discoursing at length on the merits of various baseball gloves when the young speaker is the only one who gives a shit about baseball.

If your kid immediately jumps on board and adopts beautiful table manners, well, wow. I am amazed and jealous and don't really know why you even bought this book (but thanks!). But if he is like just about every other kid in the world, you should expect a pretty steep learning curve—a curve during which your lucky self gets to walk the tough, teeny line between positive encouragement and negative consequences.

You already know that an endless stream of nagging and increasingly impatient reminders do absolutely nothing to enhance your kid's behavior in other areas, so let's just assume those tactics won't work here, either. Let's also assume that you'd like to enjoy your own dinner rather than spend your entire mealtime coaching your kid on manners and conduct. That means you need to do the following: Once your kid understands what's expected of him, institute a three-strikes rule during meals. The first time he burps or chews with his mouth open or whatever, quietly name the behavior and say, "Warning." (For example, "Napkin in the lap. Warning.")

The second time, name the behavior and say, "Strike one." The next time is strike two, and (presumably you get where I'm going here) the next is strike three, at which point he leaves the table and finishes his meal (no dessert, just what's on his plate) in a different area—a spot close enough that you can keep half an eye on him, but far enough that you can't hear his every chomp and see his every morsel of chewed-up food. You can futz with the strikes a bit if you want—skip the warning, for example, or add a consequence to strike two like losing half of his dessert—but keeping to this general system will help your kid learn to behave properly during meals with pretty minimal commentary from you.

And it will work—provided that you follow through consistently and calmly. Of course it's hard to send your kid away from the table, especially when dinner may be one of your only opportunities to connect all day and when spending time with your kid is obviously so much more important than whether he slurps his soup or not. But unless you are willing to settle for many more years of your kid handling himself at meals exactly as he does now, that's what you need to do. In my opinion, upsetting a kid and sending him away from the table a few times is infinitely more appealing than five thousand more dinners spent smiling through clenched teeth as your dining companions debate who farted first and swirl ketchup-coated fingers through their mashed potatoes—but that's really your decision. As long as you don't bring your kid to my house.

If you do adopt this plan, make sure that your behavior is up to snuff as well. When you're accustomed to your kid's lip-smacky, burpy comportment, it's easy to feel smug about your own table manners by comparison—but your kid will improve rapidly, and when he does, he may look askance at your running a finger around the edge of your pasta bowl to pick up the last vestige of sauce. (Wait, that was me. It was fantastic sauce, though.)

Please know, too, that it's not all doom and gloom around the table. A great way to head off mindless chatter before it starts is to introduce topics of conversation that will interest the whole family; you can buy decks of cards filled with suggested questions or just come up with your own. Relating your earliest memories, imagining where you'll be in ten years, describing your ideal vacation—these are all fun ways to bond with your kid in the context of relaxed, appropriate dinnertime conversation. You may even be surprised at what you'll learn; I had no idea that my son envisioned himself living in a small house by a river someday, for example, or that my daughter remembered getting in trouble for tearing up a Berenstain Bears book (long story) before she turned two. And be sure to give your kid plenty of positive feedback as his manners improve—and consider rewarding him with special desserts, dinners served on fancy dishes and eaten by candlelight, or increased input in setting the week's dinner menus. If your kid's behaving more like an adult at mealtimes, after all, he should be treated more like an adult at mealtimes.

Your kid will love hearing this, by the way—almost as much as you'll love saying it, and recognizing the truth of your words.

YOUR KID DOESN'T SAY PLEASE

◆ ◆ ◆ ◆ ◆ ◆ ◆ ◆

This happened during my first month teaching school:

A student—an adorable student, incidentally, bright and well behaved, the type who opened her book when told and threw away Kleenex she'd used instead of leaving it crumpled on the floor, presumably as a present for me to take home and cherish because she was just that awesome—anyway, this student approached my desk and said urgently, "Mrs. Glickman, I need some reinforcements."

I continued grading papers, smiling vaguely but mostly ignoring the girl. Concerned, she tried again. "Mrs. Glickman? Did you hear me? I need some reinforcements."

This time I looked up and answered calmly, "I did hear you. I'm just waiting to help you until you've spoken to me politely."

This adorable child stood there, completely stymied. She was obviously thinking hard. A moment later, she took a deep breath and said uncertainly, "I need some reinforcements now?"

I cannot even tell you how shocked I was that this sweet, personable girl did not know to say please. What can I say—it was my first teaching job! I did not yet have kids, and I had not yet made the acquaintance of what feels like four billion children—including, perhaps, your own—equally unfamiliar with the magic word. Since that fateful day I have become significantly less shockable—and much crankier.

The death of "please" must make you cranky, too—doesn't it? Or do you actually enjoy being ordered about by your offspring? Do you come alive every time your kid tells you, "I need a pen," or "Open my door"? Do you thrill to pour milk into your kid's cereal bowl when she impatiently reminds you she doesn't like her Multi Grain Cheerios dry ("Uck! That's too much milk, Mom. Can't you be *careful*?") and feel totally amazing when paying for new flip-flops she's sort of asked for/sort of demanded and in the context of which she has never uttered the word "please"?

I don't want to presume, because maybe you do like this. Maybe you think "please" is too formal, too hierarchical and imposing, and that letting "please" drift into oblivion draws you closer to your kid. Maybe you feel embarrassed reminding your kid to say please—I mean, didn't you always say please to grown-ups when you were little? Shouldn't your kid just *know*? Maybe you have limited time with your kid and want to spend it having fun together rather than instilling basic manners in her, because, you know, manners aren't fun, but doing and getting her whatever she says no matter how she says it—well, that's a total blast. And maybe you fear demanding the respect from your kid that "please" implies—maybe you think she'll just stare at you blankly or laugh or pull out that sarcastic voice you're just getting to know and use it to utter a "please" so insincere and horrible you'll never want to hear the word again.

Whatever your reason, it may seem pretty good from where you're sitting—but it's not good enough. You may be willing to forgo your kid's "please"—but the rest of the world isn't, and it will make life much better not only for them but ultimately for your kid if you start teaching her to say please. Like, right now.

Because "please" is more than just a word. (It's the magic word, right?) "Please" both instills and assumes an attitude of humility and earnestness, qualities much nicer to foster in your kid than arrogance and entitlement. When your kid says please, she implicitly acknowledges that she's not the boss, that her desires and whims are not absolute law. And saying please to anyone of whom she's making a request reminds her to treat others with respect—whether it's a teacher, a coach, the disembodied voice taking her order at the Taco Bell drive-through (don't roll your eyes at me: Taco Bell is totally amazing), or even you, her self-effacing yet wonderful parent.

There are a ton of practical benefits to your kid's "pleases" as well. So few kids have the habit these days that your kid will become a total star every time she drops a "Could you please?" I cannot tell you how many treats my kids have received on airplanes simply because they looked the flight attendant in the eye and asked, "May I please have some orange juice?" One Delta attendant dropped a truckload of those fabulous Biscoff cookies in my son's lap because his was the only "please" she'd heard all day. But even if you don't like Biscoff (gluten, yeah, I know), you—and your kid—will still like the compliments you receive from the "pleases," not to mention the favorable treatment a well-placed "please" can elicit from a teacher, a coach, or an adult considering buying your kid a gift or letting her use the single working bathroom stall at the movie theater when there's a huge line but she really, really has to go (true story!).

Yes, "please" is that great—so it should be a snap to bring your kid on board, right? Uh, sure. But just in case she doesn't instantly and cheerfully get with the program, here is a plan for instilling the "please" habit in your kid:

Like pretty much everything, "please" begins with you. At a neutral time, share briefly and matter-of-factly with your kid that as she gets older, the way she speaks to other people becomes more significant, and that you are going to work with her on making "please" a bigger part of her vocabulary. Then hold tight! When she delivers a "please"-less request—or says please in a tone that lets you know she means "I don't mean it and resent you for making me say it"—don't shame or scold her; stay calm and simply remind her to reframe her request as "Will you please help me with my math?" or "May I please play on your phone?" If she complies, that is fantastic, and you should reward her request as fully as possible; if she gives you an annoyed look or a response like, "Seriously, Mom? It's my *homework*," tell her to ask again when she's ready to say please—and occupy yourself with something else until she does.

Will this annoy your kid? Of course! But annoying your kid is part of your job description, and really, so is getting her to quit sounding like an entitled jerk. And though the beginning of this process is not necessarily easy or fun, it won't be long before you realize how wonderful it feels not to hop to your kid's every demand, to shake off the sense that you'd somehow become Cinderella to her stepmother, and to bask in the admiring looks of your friends when they hear "please" flow with (apparent) effortlessness from your kid's mouth.

A superquick note for those reading ahead: If your kid is still small, you have the most fabulous opportunity to inoculate her against this particular form of brattiness by starting now. Yes, even before she can string together a coherent sentence! Rather than teaching your kid just to say "more," "yes," and "higher," encourage her to say "more, please," "yes, please," and "higher, please." It's so easy to do when your kid is young; and while she may have no idea (yet!) what "please" means, she'll grow accustomed both to the word and to the concept of speaking a certain way in order to get what she wants. As she gets older, cue her to say please when she's asking for something: "Do you want water please or milk please?" or "Do you want to stay in the swing please or get down please?"—and remember that even a kid overwhelmed by the frustrations of putting on her own socks is not too overwhelmed to amend "I need help with my socks" to "Can you please help me with my socks?"

Now that we've taken care of your kid, let's grab one last minute to take care of you. Remember—like pretty much everything, "please" not only begins but can end with you as well. All your gentle reminders, all your walking away from "please"-less requests, all your relief and pride as "please" begins to take hold in your kid—it's ultimately all for naught unless you show your kid that "please" is important to you, too. Because if you brusquely inform your waiter, "I'll take the chicken Caesar and a Diet Coke"; if you tell the dry cleaner, "I need this pressed by Friday"; if you order your kid, "Take the dog out before it gets dark"—well, chances are great your kid will behave exactly the same way.

YOUR KID NEVER SAYS THANK YOU

◆ ◆ ◆ ◆ ◆ ◆ ◆ ◆

When I was in graduate school, my class held a coffeehouse/talent night (talent broadly defined, budding MFAs we were not) to raise money for a local food pantry. Moved by the spirit of the evening, I volunteered to be a server, which required me to move among tables crammed with fellow students and fill their orders for whole wheat pasta and artisan muffins and the occasional Coke. I did a pretty good job, if I may say so myself, but my work was apparently not up to snuff for a woman in my program, who chastised me when I brought her dessert and coffee.

"Well, that took a long time," she sniffed. "And did you use soy milk for the latte?"

At that moment I wished I had used my spit for the latte, actually, and that I had enough dramatic flair to muster a scathing reply—but alas, no MFA, remember? However, the concept of karma (at least as far as I understand it—my graduate degree was also not in Hinduism or Sanskrit) suggests that my classmate eventually encountered someone who did, and that her thanklessness was met with the response it deserved.

Why am I relating this long-ago incident? In part because I'm hoping my antagonist will read this and contact me to apologize (no, it's okay, seriously, especially because I had in fact forgotten the soy)—although mostly because I fear your kid is headed down the exact same path trodden by my classmate. But there's still time to salvage your kid's karmic destiny by teaching her to use those two magnificent words: "thank you."

Of course your kid is already familiar with the phrase thank-you, because she hears it just about every minute of the day. Honestly, how often does thank-you fall from your lips? Your kid hands you a used tissue. "Thank you!" Your kid brushes her teeth after, like, the fortieth time you've reminded her to do so, plus squeezed watermelon Colgate onto her electric brush. "Thank you!" Your kid finds your unattended phone and takes it upon herself to change your wallpaper to a picture of Ariana Grande. "Thank you!" But your kid is probably only dimly aware that she's supposed to say thank you as well, particularly when someone has actually done something nice for her—and it's time for that to change.

Of course you've heard a million times that parenting is a thankless job—but it doesn't have to be that way. While it's delusional to expect an infant to thank you for wiping her poopy bottom or reading her a story (unless your kid is just that advanced, and yes, I totally believe you that she is), it's also pretty ridiculous to continue this dynamic throughout the years that follow. There's nothing morally superior about toiling endlessly for your school-age kid and telling yourself that the only thanks you need is seeing your kid healthy and happy. I mean, really, don't be such a sap. It's okay to admit that you want your kid to appreciate and offer thanks for the stuff you do—not that you necessarily need a thank-you every time you make something she likes for dinner (though that may come in time), but certainly your patient attempts to explain adding fractions and your heroic drive through rush-hour traffic to take your kid to rehearsal should be met not with a blank stare or a halfhearted wave good-bye but with a grateful smile and an enthusiastic thank-you, you know?

Because that thank-you is so much more than two simple words. It's an acknowledgment of the time and the energy you devote to your kid, and it's an assurance that your efforts are noticed and valued. It's also a recognition that you're more than an automaton programmed to attend to your kid's needs and desires—you're a thinking, feeling human being who deserves positive feedback every now and then. And finally, it's a way to increase your kid's respect for you and to improve your interactions; after all, a kid who has learned to look you in the eye and offer a sincere thank-you for a visit to the ice-cream parlor is a kid much less likely to complain that she was not allowed a second scoop or a topping.

And you're not the only one who deserves a thank-you from time to time. Even if you're hesitant about accepting thanks for the nice things you do for your kid (which you absolutely should not be; I mean, seriously), the rest of the world is eager to hear your kid say thank you, particularly when your kid has just been handed a piece of gum or given a cut in line at a public bathroom or perhaps hosted for a totally awesome playdate featuring water balloons and homemade ice pops, both of which somehow found their way into my dining room mere hours after the cleaning lady had left—but I digress. A hearty thank-you can make all the difference in how others view your kid—grateful versus greedy, polite versus pushy, a welcome guest versus an entry on the off-site-playdates-only list—and how she's treated when she ventures outside her adoring home. I have personally seen a sweetly uttered thank-you rewarded with a free bag of fried Oreos (don't judge until you've tried them; they are truly worth the five years they'll take off your life); the chance to hold a fresh-from-the-awesome-3D-printer model of a dinosaur skull at the Museum of Natural History in Washington, D.C.; a Japanese fan (long story); an open invitation to spend the night at a friend's lake house; and an extra ten minutes of Xbox when it was so time to go to bed. Honestly, people want to be nicer, to do more, to go above and beyond for someone who appears to appreciate their efforts—and why shouldn't that someone be your kid?

But the swag isn't even the most important part. Not to sound totally corny, but instilling the "thank you" habit in your kid will ultimately yield all kinds of wonderful life lessons. Our society focuses so much on go, go, go and get, get, get that it's rare to find an opportunity just to sit back and enjoy where we are and what we've got. We're also much better at yearning and complaining than accepting and appreciating, and we're awfully focused on material acquisitions and keeping up with the "haves" around us. And while I'm not promising that regularly saying thank you will inoculate your kid against these pernicious messages, well, it actually sort of will. A kid taught to say thank you for a small gift is a kid who pauses to take stock of what she has and to look upon it with gratitude. A kid taught to say thank you for a trip to the zoo is a kid who envisions special treats not as an entitlement but as a privilege. A kid taught to say thank you for an invitation to a party is a kid who will—at least for a moment—admire her surroundings before tearing into a goody bag or cramming a slice of birthday cake into her mouth. And while even a kid taught to say thank you is going to want and whine far more than you might like, she's also far more likely to thoughtfully consider than sneeringly dismiss your gentle reminder to take pleasure in what she already has. Simply put, "thank you" teaches your kid what's called an attitude of gratitude—and really, who couldn't use a little more of that?

The journey from your grabby, thankless kid to this mini Zen master is not a short one—but as Lao-tzu taught, "A journey of a thousand miles begins with a single step." (No graduate degree in Chinese philosophy, either, just a brief dalliance with a Taoist, like, a million years ago.) And the first step is introducing your kid to her obligation to say thank you whenever someone does something nice for her: "It was polite of that man to hold the door open for us. That's why I told him thank-you, and next time, you should say it, too." "I'm happy to make dinners you like, and I think you like it when I do. Be sure you remember to tell me thank-you—it lets me know that you appreciate what I do, and it makes me feel good." "Brianna's mom was sweet enough to take you girls to the movies and buy you popcorn? You are so lucky! Please look her in the eye and give her a big thank-you before you leave." Don't do this in a shaming, impatient manner—your kid has probably lived a thank-you–free life for many years now, so she'll need a little while to get in the swing of things—but don't act as if she's accomplished something amazing every time she utters the phrase, and don't let her get away with muttering a half-assed thank-you because she's supposedly overtired, bashful, or cranky. Also don't shy away from providing logical, meaningful consequences as necessary; from being required to write thank-you notes within forty-eight hours of receiving gifts to losing a dessert for defiantly refusing to say thank you, your kid may need a bit of tough love to understand the importance of thank-you—and to realize how serious you are about this new initiative.

Another step is to make sure you're practicing what you preach. One of the most effective ways to get your kid to say thank you is to say it a lot yourself. You may be surprised at how difficult this step can be; when you're in a rush (usually), preoccupied (always), or in a bad mood (more often than you'd like), thank-you is one of the first things to fall by the wayside. It's also shamefully easy to forget to say thank you to people in the service industries: the guy fixing your SUV, the woman grooming your dog, the teenager mangling your order at the deli (Only two of the bagels were supposed to be sliced! How can you possibly be out of reduced-fat cream cheese?—I mean, thank you!), but remembering to do so will set a great example for your kid, as well as make you a better person in general. And if you're an overachiever—or maybe just really nice—you can take things to the next level, say, by dropping off cookies at the local fire station or approaching a soldier in the airport to thank him or her for serving our country. Your kid may act totally embarrassed the first time or two you do this, but I almost promise that pretty soon, she'll be right by your side.

Finally, remember the point of the journey: to make "thank you" a major part of your kid's life. If you remain consistent, firm, and positive, you'll be delighted with how quickly this happens—and with the incredible difference it will make in your kid's behavior, outlook, and general personality. A fabulous side effect is that you will feel like the best parent in the world—seriously, wait till an entire shift of employees start falling all over themselves praising your child-rearing skills because your kid actually thanked the person who gave her a free sample of salted caramel frozen yogurt (true story!). Just don't forget to thank them for the compliments, okay?

YOUR KID IS TOTALLY RUDE TO GROWN-UPS

◆ ◆ ◆ ◆ ◆ ◆ ◆ ◆

When your kid was a toddler, the grown-ups descending on him with broad smiles and open arms totally understood when your kid ran away or buried his face in your shoulder. (And if they didn't, they're jerks—I mean, really.) Even when your kid made it to preschool, he got a pass for looking away when an adult addressed him or for shrugging wordlessly when someone asked him what he wanted to be when he grew up or if he liked his baby brother or something equally tedious.

But as you may have noticed, your kid has grown—and behaviors that used to inspire understanding nods and affectionate pats on the head (also tedious) are now triggering impatience, annoyance, and general exasperation. This is not because the adults interacting with your kid have suddenly morphed into assholes who demand perfect manners and impeccable social graces far beyond his tender years—it's simply because they would like for your school-age kid to return their greetings or to look them in the eye or to treat them with a modicum of courtesy and respect. And not to insult your kid—he's the one holding the serving bowl of pretzels on his lap and not glancing up when people tell him hello and comment on how big and handsome he's grown, right?—but they kind of have a point.

I know, I know: Your kid is shy and reserved, far too timid to comply with these expectations. He's also just a kid, come on—there's plenty of time for him to master the niceties of etiquette when he's older. (How much older? one might ask. Well, how are you supposed to know? Just, like, older.) Plus, your kid is most comfortable spending time with people he knows well, with those embracing souls who accept his true self and don't try to mold him into some "how do you do, sir, and may I take your coat, ma'am" automaton. To put it plainly, your kid Doesn't Do Well Around Strangers, and people need to honor that.

To all this, I—and most of the people who encounter your kid—respond: Hmmm.

Yes, you have a point. After all, our child-revering culture is eager to completely absolve your kid of any responsibility for making nice with adults and to put the onus on grown-ups to find common ground with your kid's generation. Add that to your constant fear of smothering your kid's unique gifts and shredding his self-esteem by suggesting he may have some room for improvement, plus a general hesitation to burden your kid with unpleasant demands, and voila! You have made an excellent case for leaving your kid alone, at least until he needs a refill on the pretzels and maybe a glass of water, and not expecting him to smile and engage with the boring adults arrayed before him.

But before we dismiss them completely, let's take a closer look at these dull, irritating grown-ups with whom your kid can't possibly be bothered. Plenty of them are shy and reserved, plenty prefer being with people they know well, and plenty (including me) do not relish time spent with strangers, particularly strangers determined to engage me in a friendly chat when I have just downloaded *The Girl on the Train* (I know, I'm the last person in the universe to read it) to my Kindle or have just figured out how to totally kick my sister's ass in Words With Friends. And not to be mean, but plenty of them don't even care how your kid's hockey season is going or genuinely notice that he's grown since the last time they saw him. So why are they going out of their way to greet your kid, to smile at him, to try to engage him in a bit of friendly conversation?

Believe it or not, these adults are not out to aggravate your kid. They are just trying to uphold the basic social expectations that exist among the human beings of this world as to how we treat one another: expectations that we say hi, that we smile, that we share a few pleasant words; expectations that we not ignore or rebuff a cheerful hello, that we not meet attempts at polite small talk with a blank face, that we not stuff our mouths with yet another handful of pretzels and return to the business of inspecting the dreck on the bottom of our shoes while our would-be conversation partners ask if we are going to camp again this summer. And as irksome as they might be, these expectations totally benefit your kid—otherwise I'd have grabbed the pretzels from him twenty minutes ago, bought myself a new pair of earbuds instead of getting him a gift card to Best Buy on his last birthday, and interrupted his monologue on his new hamster to show off my awesome pedicure—and he should start fulfilling a few himself.

Hopefully you know me well enough by now to assume the following, but in case you just opened the book for the first time and landed on this page: If your kid has genuine issues, social anxiety, attachment disorders, a place on the autism spectrum, or something along those lines, of course I am not talking to you. But there are many, many kids out there who—according to their besotted parents—should not be held accountable for displaying manners or observing basic conventions of behavior, when the only thing truly standing between these kids and social skills are overindulgent and coddling adults. Here's a quick way to determine where your kid lies: If you are convinced he's a retiring hothouse flower, but he seems to have no problem informing a waitress that she forgot his fries, accepting a generous gift from a family friend, or explaining at length to an incredibly patient audience what he is constructing on Minecraft, then please read on.

Of course this is a gradual process, and believe me, no one is anticipating Emily Post when they decide to converse with your kid. But the best way for your kid to start developing basic manners is for you to stop making excuses for what he can't do and instead focus on what he can and should. So please, take the pretzels away already, and consider introducing your kid to these rudimentary expressions of polite behavior. And would it kill him to sit up straight?

Stand up when an adult enters the room. Yes, I am totally serious. This is so easy for your kid to do, and so utterly charming. It may seem like an insanely outdated custom, but adults (especially older adults) remember it well and will deeply appreciate seeing it revived. Plus, it goes a long way toward instilling respect for grown-ups, which might serve your kid well. Just saying.

Smile and shake hands. Unless your kid is pathologically shy or the adult is dripping with phlegm, your kid should greet adults by smiling, looking them in the eye, and extending his hand. Even though this practice may sound awkward, it actually helps shy or uncertain kids immensely by providing them with a script and a step-by-step plan for handling social encounters. It is also far superior to, say, muttering, grunting, or perhaps growling upon being introduced to one's parent's friend from out of town. (True story! Although the growling child was, her mother helpfully explained, upset because she could not find her Rainbow Loom and was just expressing her frustration. Oh. Okay.)

Put other people first. A major part of polite behavior is demonstrating consideration for others, which in practice boils down to not going first and insisting on the best all the fucking time. This means teaching your kid to hold the door open for adults rather than pushing past them and scooching through (yeah, grown-ups are slow, sorry), standing up to offer an adult his seat instead of staying put while someone nine times your kid's age looks around in vain for a place to rest her weary bones, and not starting an extremely noisy empty-wrapping-paper-tube fight with three similarly high-spirited buddies, like, ten feet away from a group of ladies complaining about their husbands over coffee and mixed-berry streusel. (Which is better than it sounds.)

Manage a conversation. The anatomy of a conversation between an adult and your kid should not consist of increasingly desperate/impatient/ridiculous attempts to get your kid to talk (from the adult) and silence/"huh?"/"yeah"/"uh"/ more silence (from your kid). Knowing how to manage a conversation with a grown-up is tremendously important—and empowering—for your kid. Teaching your kid how to nod politely, hold up his end of the conversation (the words "Really?" and "Wow" will serve him well), and make a clean getaway ("That's so interesting! Please excuse me, I think my mom needs me") will not only make him a more considerate and well-mannered person, but will also enable him to handle uncomfortable situations with confidence and (appropriate) self-assertiveness.

These behaviors are just the beginning—but holy shit, what a great beginning. And while instilling these manners in your kid will not be a total snap, your firm and consistent guidance, plus the lavish praise and positive attention your kid will garner from his efforts, will make the process a lot easier than you are imagining. And the payoff is fantastic for everyone—for the adults interacting with your kid, for sure, but also for your now-infinitely-more-socialized-and-secure kid and for you, the parent whom every grown-up in a hundred-mile radius now thinks of as the best ever.

Trust me: Once your kid has mastered these skills, you will start noticing how they set him apart—and you will look with exasperation at the hordes of clueless parents who let their kids get away with less. Just don't expect to chat about this phenomenon with me for too long; I'm fine with exchanging friendly smiles and a bit of small talk, but after a couple of minutes, I'll be sneaking away ("That's so interesting! Please excuse me, I think my kid needs me") to read *The Girl on the Train* in the bathroom.

YOUR KID LIES

◆ ◆ ◆ ◆ ◆ ◆ ◆ ◆

Everybody lies once in a while, right? But that doesn't mean your kid should lie. Especially not to you.

I know, I know: It's important to be understanding. To foster an atmosphere of safety and unconditional love. To give your kid the amazing gifts of trust and wholehearted acceptance.

This all sounds fantastic. But it works only if your kid doesn't—how can I put it delicately—turn into a complete and total liar.

It starts so innocently. You've told your kid no cookie before lunch—and ten minutes later, lo and behold, the bag of cookies is no longer in its usual spot in the pantry. Also, your kid is uncharacteristically quiet and withdrawn. Also, there are crumbs on her chin.

What are you supposed to do? Obviously, she's snagged a cookie without permission; and as the parent, you must Deal With It. So you kneel down to her level, make eye contact, and ask solemnly, "Honey, did you take a cookie?"

Your little sweetheart pushes her lower lip out, trembles, looks away. In a barely audible, half-pleading voice, she whispers, "No."

No? What the fuck? Of course she took the cookie! But oh my gosh, she's so little and sweet and clearly ashamed—and you certainly don't want to shame your precious girl, do you? So you purse your lips and say gently, "Sweetie, are you sure you didn't take a cookie?"

Now your kid can almost look you in the eye. Somehow she's gotten both the cookie and the upper hand, and she's happy to help herself to both. "No!" she replies, voice a little stronger this time, back a little straighter. "No! I didn't."

Well, what are you supposed to do at this point? Call your own kid a liar? Triumphantly present your evidence, then watch her face crumple as she realizes her own parent has set a trap for her? Or mumble that, well, you're not sure what happened, but she is definitely not to have cookies before lunch, and you don't want this to happen again, okay? Okay.

None of these options is all that great, but you've probably chosen the third. Which seemed like a good idea at the time. You avoided a confrontation, you made your point (you think), and—even though you didn't actually say anything to this effect—you taught your kid the importance of telling the truth by letting her feel the discomfort and unpleasantness that come with lying.

So if things have gone so well, why do you feel kind of lousy? And maybe like you let your kid off too easy for, you know, *totally lying to your face*?

Here's the thing: Truth telling may seem less important when we're confronted with the eyes of an embarrassed child, the specter of a stressful confrontation, a rush of unpleasant emotions like guilt and anger and disappointment. But it's actually at these moments that honesty is most important. When we shy away from instilling this value in our kids, we fail them in a terrible way. And as much as we may hate to use words like "lie" and "dishonest" in conjunction with our beloved children, there's simply no other way to salvage terms like "truth" and "trust."

Yes, there are plenty of understandable, developmentally appropriate reasons for your kid to lie: She's saying what she wishes were true, she's afraid of disappointing or angering you, she's not one hundred percent clear on this whole truth-telling thing. None of these reasons, however, means her lying is actually okay. And it's up to you to explain this to her—ideally the first time she experiments with fibbing.

First, some reassurance: Contrary to popular belief, calling your kid out on a lie is not the same thing as demolishing her self-esteem. We've become terrified of telling our kids, "I don't believe you"—even when we're totally positive they're lying to us—for fear of making them "feel bad" or causing them to experience discomfort or humiliation. But guess what? When your kid lies, she should feel bad—and your primary focus should not be on immediately making her feel better but on exploring why she feels bad, and teaching her not to make lying a habit.

The type of lie you may shrink from reacting to—one from a child with crumbs on her face denying she took a cookie, a kid with marker-smeared hands saying she wasn't the one who drew on the wall, a pie-eyed and clearly petrified seven-year-old promising she didn't sneak downstairs to get a peek at the *American Horror Story: Hotel* episode you were watching after she'd gone to bed—are actually the best lies to confront. The stakes are relatively low, your kid is young and (mostly) eager to please, and there's still plenty of time to revisit and practice the value of honesty. So grab the opportunity! When your kid lies to you, don't let the lie pass—but also don't freak out or yell or launch into a diatribe about how you know the truth. Give your kid your full attention, and say quietly but firmly, "You just lied to me," "That doesn't sound like the truth to me," or something similar. Keep your reaction simple and brief, and keep your eyes on your kid while you talk. She'll look uncomfortable and kind of miserable, which is actually a good thing in this case, so keep it up. Tell her, "Lying is a bad thing to do, and it makes people feel bad. You feel bad when you lie, and people feel bad when you lie to them. When you lie to people, they can't trust you or believe what you say. Sometimes people lie because they don't want to get into trouble, but lying is worse than getting into trouble." Just sit with your kid for a while and let her absorb what you've said; you can put your arm around her or give her a hug, but don't start a bunch of soothing noises like "It's okay, sweetie, it's okay." If your kid starts arguing or pleading her case, don't engage; just respond, "I hear that you want me to believe you, but people can't believe you when you lie."

Of course you've still got the original transgression to deal with—and even if your kid seems beyond remorseful, don't let that go. Give her an appropriate consequence, and use it to remind her that lying makes everything worse: "Since you already ate a cookie, there's no cookie after lunch. But since you also lied about it, there's no cookie after dinner, either," or "Since you drew on the wall, you'll need to clean it up. Since you also lied about it, I'm only going to help you for one minute instead of helping you with the whole thing."

Believe it or not, these encounters—difficult as they may be—are actually a great gift for your kid. It does feel terrible to lie, especially to people we love, and helping your kid realize that while she's still young is superimportant. By calling her out on her lie, you also strengthen your authority, ease her guilty conscience, and remind her of the importance of honesty—it's win-win-win. And you have a fantastic opportunity to emphasize this value in the days ahead; give your kid lots of chances to tell the truth (easy stuff like "Are you watching TV?" when you've already given permission and she clearly is)—and praise her honesty when she does.

You can also discourage your kid's burgeoning attraction to lying by being a little more straightforward yourself. One of the bigger reasons school-age kids lie is that they're trying to get out of trouble; if you remove that tantalizing possibility, you'll also remove a major incentive to lie. Next time you know your kid's done something sneaky or wrong, don't play games or set a trap; if you see your kid dumping vegetables from her dinner plate into her lap, don't ask, "Honey, are you eating your healthy food first?" Just tell her to knock it off. Really, your kid's giving you enough trouble as it is—why go begging for more by tempting her to lie?

I do feel compelled to confess that this is one of those chapters that's easier to write than to live. Not that writing a book is the simplest thing in the world; but in many ways, it's a lot less demanding than staring a kid you love in the eye and calling her out on a lie. But there's really no other good choice. Let's face it: Lying is appealing on a lot of levels; being honest is really hard; and telling the truth when the truth might get you into trouble is not all that fun. It's up to you to set your kid on the right path; not to freak you out completely, but your lying kid is not going to magically morph into an upright person of integrity without your doing some tough work.

And as tough as this work is, it's totally worthwhile. Every bit as worthwhile as being honest even when—in the short term, anyway—a lie might serve you better.

YOUR KID HAS AN OBNOXIOUS BEST FRIEND

◆ ◆ ◆ ◆ ◆ ◆ ◆ ◆

Yay that your kid is developing socially, that she's forging connections with her peers, that she's finding people-who-are-not-you to play endless rounds of Clue Jr. and talk about *Jessie* with. You remember those amazing, heady days of life with a best friend, and you're so excited for your kid. You're excited for yourself, too—ready to be the fun mom basking in happy oohs and aahs as you present your kid and her friend with a plateful of snacks, listening to the whispers and giggles rising from the backseat as you drive them to the trampoline park, finally finding appreciative recipients for the eight candy-colored bridesmaid dresses that have languished in the back of your closet since 2005. This is going to be fantastic!

Until you meet your kid's new best friend. And realize she's *horrible*.

Of course on one level you realize this is just cosmic payback for the disasters of favored companions you foisted on your own parents. I will confess to cultivating the friendship of a second grade girl I'll call Andrea, because that was her name, and I seriously cannot imagine she will ever read this because she is probably in prison by now. Anyway, the first time Andrea came to my house, she sucked on a bottle of Elmer's glue as if it were a baby bottle for, like, an hour, then whapped my preschool-age brother over the head with a wooden mallet from his play xylophone. The best part for my parents? I thought Andrea was fantastic and begged to have her over again the following week, by which point the bump on my brother's head would surely have improved (I believe I actually pointed this out, certain it would bolster my cause). What a delight that must have been!

So if you had an Andrea in your early life—and who didn't?—your kid's obnoxious best friend may be karmic vengeance. But understanding that fact, uttering a silent apology to the universe (or in my case my brother, who strangely has grown up to be far more together and successful than I, his uninjured sister), and recognizing that your kid is going to pick a few jerks along her road to social independence will take you only so far. You're still stuck between a kid you can't stand and your own kid, whom you love more than life itself and who's joyfully proclaiming this interloper to be her best friend forever. What are you going to do?

Well, it depends. First, take a deep breath and give the friend a chance. You know how you're always telling your kid not to judge someone by how they look or by their first impression, and that what's really important about people is what's on the inside? Make sure you're taking your own advice. Of course you're envisioning your kid seated among the popular group, and of course you realize that having a best friend who picks her nose when she thinks no one's looking (but they must be—*you've* seen her do it eight times already) is not really a step in that direction, but guess what? That may not be your kid's concern at all, she may already know that the popular group's not for her, or she may have looked past the nose picking and found a really kind, fun friend who enjoys her company and makes her feel good about herself. If this is the case, you can skip the rest of the chapter and go take a candlelit bubble bath; you're bringing up an open-minded, nonjudgmental kid, and—as long as you can follow her example and demonstrate these qualities yourself—you've earned a little reward.

But what if it's not just a matter of looking beneath the surface? Well, then, you have some work to do. Assuming the words "annoying," "irritating," and "unpleasant" better describe the friend than "menacing," "sociopathic," and "knife-wielding"—and if your kid has truly bonded with a menacing, knife-wielding sociopath, you may want to look into switching schools—you're about to embark on a new and challenging path. Walking the line among honoring your kid's need to choose her own friends, fostering independence and self-confidence in her social skills, and guiding her to surround herself with good people who genuinely like her and who bring out her best is kind of like tightroping across the Grand Canyon, except maybe without a rope.

So before you jump in with judgments and plans, do a little research. Of course it's hard to watch your kid spend time with this obnoxious child, but try to remain detached and determine exactly why you object to the friendship. You might want to pretend you're an anthropologist observing the social behavior of some exotic tribe; I know it sounds ridiculous, but it actually helps! Ask yourself questions and investigate the answers: Does the friend show disrespect and rudeness? Under what circumstances? At whom does she direct her behavior? Does her behavior influence your kid? Or, is the friend more socially mature than your kid? What language, behaviors, or aspects of popular culture is she introducing to your kid? Which specific elements do you find disturbing? How is your kid reacting? Considering the particular problems with the friendship will help you respond effectively, and it may also keep you within the bounds of acceptable discourse; calling a second grade girl "insufferable" or "loathsome" makes you look kind of insufferable and loathsome yourself—but airing your concern that your kid is being negatively influenced by an offensive peer, well, that makes you look like a concerned and proactive parent.

Once you've figured out the specific problem your kid's new bestie is causing, you can design an appropriate course of action. If your kid comes home overstimulated and hyper after spending time with the friend, for example, you can require that she take twenty minutes of downtime in her room after a playdate. If the friend is sassy, and your kid is starting to imitate this less-than-charming behavior, call your kid on it and institute a three-strikes rule: Three episodes of rude behavior after a playdate mean no playdate next time. If your kid comes home from playdates whining about how much bigger her friend's house is and how much better her friend's snacks are, try not to react as if it's a personal attack (though it feels lousy, I know, believe me, I've been there)—just tell her matter-of-factly that you're glad she had such a good time and that if she could wash up and set the table, that would be really outstanding.

A final warning: Don't assume that your kid's occasional bumbling in selecting friends means you'd do any better. Of course the nose-picking friend, the insanely loud and overactive friend, the entitled and spoiled friend, the sassy and back-talking friend aren't going to be high on your list—but they may actually be better for your kid than the friend you wish she had. Yes, I know the one—the pretty little girl who's always surrounded by giggling companions at carline, the one who wins the election for student council representative and has her artwork displayed in the hall and looks you in the eye to say thank you when you volunteer in the classroom—and, inexplicably, the one your kid refuses to invite for a playdate and won't go near during recess. Please give your kid some respect, and some space, on this one. It may be that your kid's just intimidated by Superfriend, that she's just not that into her, or that you're one hundred percent right and your kid is missing out on the most fabulous pal ever—but it may also be that behind that adorable smile, sweet little Superfriend is actually the meanest girl in the class, and your kid has every reason to stay away.

If you think I'm being ridiculous, you have clearly never met my former student Genevieve (not her real name; I am terrified of her to this day), who charmed every adult in school with her beautiful manners and excellent grades and always-tucked-in uniform blouse—and who revealed her true colors only once, when I assigned her to work on a group project with poor little Erika. Genevieve earnestly informed me—in Erika's earshot!—that Erika was really not Genevieve's "style" of person and could Erika please be, "you know, moved away"?

So when you think you've found the holy grail of friends for your kid—please think of Genevieve and back off. Don't override your kid's opinions and tell your kid who's nice—because they are not always nice. I know you're savvy, I know you've seen *Mean Girls* and read *Odd Girl Out* and *Queen Bees and Wannabes* and *Little Girls Can Be Mean* and maybe even *Cat's Eye*, I know you can tell who's for real and who's not, and of course I know that you won't be fooled by a seven-year-old mean girl . . . except that, well, you will.

YOUR KID WON'T DO HIS HOMEWORK

◆ ◆ ◆ ◆ ◆ ◆ ◆ ◆

This is one of my husband's favorite jokes:

Leonard wakes up sulky and refuses to get out of bed. "Leonard!" his mother cries, aflutter and anxious. "You must get out of bed!"

Leonard turns to face the wall. "Why?"

"Why? Because you have to go to school!"

"I hate school! The teachers are mean, the kids are mean, and nobody likes me."

"Still, Leonard, you must go to school!"

"Why?"

"Why? Because, Leonard—you're the *principal*!"

Isn't that the best joke? And doesn't it remind you of the fun hours you and your kid are spending together these days?

"I don't want to do homework! It's stupid, it's hard, and it ruins the entire night!"

"Still, you must do homework!"

"Why?"

"Why? Because—you're the *parent*!"

How did this happen, anyway? You finished elementary school a while ago, right? (Actually, a really long while ago, but let's not think about that; it gets depressing.) You've probably earned at least one diploma since then, you've almost stopped having those anxiety dreams where you walk into a class you've never attended before and are presented with a test you can't comprehend, and you are totally over carrying thirty pounds of textbooks on your back while trying to look fetching and carefree every time Greg Tharp passes you in the hallway (wait, that was me). So why are you stressing out about fourth grade homework every single night?

Because your kid is completely stressed out, of course! He's overwhelmed with homework, and who can blame him? He works hard all day at school, then comes home exhausted, needing to relax and recharge in the bosom of his loving family—but instead faces a mountain of math problems, endless sheets of language arts exercises, a chapter book, and who knows what else. He's cranky, he's fussy, he's unable to focus on his assignments—and he needs you by his side, soothing and comforting and offering a constant stream of encouragement and hints and tips on Staying Calm and You Can Do It and Keeping Yourself Organized.

Unless, well, maybe not.

Now, I understand some kids are truly overwhelmed by homework. Learning differences that require assistance and interventions, a genuinely bad teacher who somehow expects his students to figure out at home what he was unable to teach coherently in class, accelerated or honors classes that require elementary schoolers to work at the level of middle school students, and two horrible words—science fair—are all occasions for significant parental concern and involvement. But please pardon me for asking if these issues truly apply to your kid. Yes, I hear him saying he's totally stressed out. I see him getting up in frustration every few minutes from the delightful little workstation you set up on what used to be your dining room table. I recognize that his apparent inability to focus, his procrastination, and his grouching could be signs that he feels besieged by homework and that the resulting pressure and anxiety could be way, way too much for him.

But I have to say that your kid looked pretty happy and engaged at soccer practice this afternoon. (Good try on that block, by the way!) He also seemed relaxed and content during dinner, at least once you remembered that he hates spinach and brought out the baby carrots and ranch dressing instead, and practically gleeful once you agreed (finally!) to some screen time even though he still had homework to do, because, well, you can't remember why, but he made a good point. It's really just since you reminded him to start his homework that his mood has taken such a turn, which of course may be a total coincidence, but well, maybe not.

Here's the thing: Your kid is still your baby, yes, but he's not a baby in general. He's old enough for soccer, for choking-hazard-before-age-four carrots, and for a school experience that doesn't begin and end with circle time. And that means he's old enough not only for homework—but also for learning to manage the stress that comes along with it.

Nor is your kid's school ridiculous and mean for recognizing this fact and acting accordingly. Your kid's teacher is not sadistic for assigning twenty math problems and a two-paragraph essay on an American president—if anything, she's a total masochist because she now has to read a stack of two-paragraph essays about said American president, and correct your kid's atrocious spelling of "inauguration" to boot. Seriously, we expect (rightfully) a lot from our schools—and their delivering means their delivering some homework as well.

And speaking of homework, it's time to recognize whose responsibility that two-paragraph essay actually is. At the moment, I realize, it feels like yours. But it doesn't have to be that way.

Homework is not really between you and your kid, or between your kid and life at home. Homework is really between your kid and school; and while behaving accordingly isn't all that popular these days, it's unbelievably liberating—for you and for your kid. Because as much as you hate standing over him criticizing his handwriting, reminding him to check his work, trying to remember how to calculate the area of a triangle so you can make sure he's Getting It Right, your kid hates it, too. And even if he's asking you to help, he's also sort of hating how quickly and fervently and thoroughly you jump to his aid; yes, you're responding and supporting him, but you're also sending the message that he's not up to the job and reinforcing his fears that he's unable to handle his schoolwork—and maybe other, more significant tasks—on his own.

So what should you do instead? Well, I'm not advising you to back off completely. If you leave your kid to his own devices, he'll either freak out all night or push his homework aside in favor of chilling out with a box of Cheez-Its and an episode of *Family Guy* (which, by the way, you should never, never let your school-age kid watch on a plane while you are trying to take a snooze—it's too late for me, but maybe not for you). And you absolutely have a responsibility to support your kid's school and teachers by showing him that homework matters. But there is a happy medium between blowing off your kid's work and letting it become the centerpiece of life at home—a happy medium that not only will make your evenings a lot less sucky but will even help your kid develop some useful study skills and an appreciation for time management.

First, help your kid set up a time and place to do his homework. Maybe it's at the kitchen table with a snack, maybe it's at his desk after supper—whatever works best for your family. And if you are having trouble figuring out a time and place for your kid to do homework besides "after basketball" and "while eating a late dinner in the back of the SUV"—well, please do consider the possibility that your kid's stress doesn't stem entirely from having to read a *Scholastic* article about Martin Luther King Jr. and finish a map skills exercise that was assigned last Tuesday.

The time and place for doing homework aren't as important as the fact that doing homework becomes part of your kid's routine, so stick to whatever you decide; don't let your kid put homework off because he's having fun with his siblings for once, because he dawdled over dinner and needs to digest, or even because he just offered to walk the dog, which is admittedly amazing and very hard to pass up. Go over briefly with your kid what homework he needs to complete, help him decide how long it should take, set a timer for that amount of time, say something encouraging . . . and walk away. Seriously, do it! When he's reaching the last five or ten minutes of homework time, you can offer a reminder—but otherwise, do your own thing and let your kid do his.

And when the timer goes off . . . that means homework gets put away. Either he did it or he didn't, but either way time is up, and the rest of your evening should be unencumbered by homework battles or histrionics. Yes, if he was goofing off or resenting his work instead of doing it, or just having trouble staying focused and managing his time, he may have consequences to face at school tomorrow—but it's far more logical for him to be disciplined at school by his teacher than cajoled or hassled by you. It's better, too; your kid's teacher will be able to give a reasonable consequence for missing homework—staying in at recess, for example, or serving a lunch detention—that will have a far more logical impact than your threatening not to take him to Eli's birthday party if he doesn't sit down right now and read *The Magic Half* for another seven minutes, you're counting! (If your kid doesn't shape up quickly enough for his teacher's taste and she asks for your support, however, feel free to keep him home from Eli's party—Eli's probably a bad influence, anyway.)

While no one dreams of being the parent sending a less-than-totally-prepared kid to school, it's far better to do it now when the stakes are relatively low than to continue coddling him and setting you both up for a rude awakening during the tween and teen years. If you don't believe me, ask a friend of mine who managed her kid's homework load all through elementary and middle school, then began her career as mom of a high schooler by e-mailing her kid's math teacher to complain (I believe the word she used was "share") that her kid had had trouble with that night's homework assignment. The teacher printed out the e-mail the next day, tossed it on the kid's desk, and told the kid, "If you have a problem with homework, you come to me. But you tell your mother Never. To. E-mail. Me. Again." Welcome to ninth grade, honey!

YOUR KID IS WASTEFUL

◆ ◆ ◆ ◆ ◆ ◆ ◆ ◆

Okay, this may sound like the beginning of a pointless rant, but please stay with me as I describe yet one more thing that drives me completely insane: kids doodling on pristine sheets of clean white paper.

I know! I sound ridiculous. Your kid wants to draw, and that's awesome. You should totally encourage her to draw—it's a great form of self-expression, it promotes imagination and creativity, it enhances motor skills and spatial relations, and for once she's not burying her nose in the Justice catalog or begging to FaceTime with Julia when they just saw each other, like, two hours ago. So what problem could there possibly be with handing your kid some colored pencils and a stack of white paper?

Well, if she's genuinely concentrating on her work, if she's putting forth her absolute best effort, if she's committed to creating something truly special, then there's no problem at all. But if she's just kind of goofing around, getting bored or annoyed with one sketch and grabbing a fresh sheet of paper to start a new one, or generating a list of new and improved ways to spell her name (Abigale! Abbey! Abi!) rather than the boring one you stuck her with at birth (Abby, really, Mom? What were you thinking?)—in that case, may I suggest that you set aside the sheets she's using and hand her a stack of scrap paper instead?

This might seem dumb—after all, who cares what kind of paper your kid uses to draw, especially when you paid for it and are thrilled to see her enjoying it? But giving your kid scrap paper for doodling is actually one of the smartest—and easiest—things you can do to instill a host of great values in your kid.

Here's what I mean: We've all heard the earth is kind of in crisis, right? And while they may not be driving electric cars or biking to work or installing solar panels on their roofs, aren't most of the good-hearted people you know making an effort to decrease their carbon footprint, recycle, save the polar bears, and all that? Well, it's time for you and your kid to step up as well.

Of course there's no possible better use of Earth's resources than supporting your kid. The only problem is that millions of other parents feel the same way about their own kids—which means an epidemic of wastefulness is upon us. It's ironic, because your kid is part of a generation that possesses more knowledge and professes more concern about the state of our planet than any other—but she's also part of a generation for whom "going without" and "making do" are largely foreign concepts.

Think about the message your kid receives when you automatically hand her fresh white paper for drawing, and when she tosses it aside as she wishes. Then think about the message you send by asking her if she's in the mood to create a really special drawing or if she just wants to doodle and sketch a little—and by directing her to a nicely maintained stack of scrap paper if she answers the latter. There is absolutely no downside, and there are so many positives: You've initiated a conversation (brief, but still a conversation!) and expressed interest in her plans, you've modeled the values of conservation and reusing, you've provided her with appropriate materials for making art, and—best of all—you've given her the opportunity to reflect on how what she wants intersects with the larger good. Plus, she's still distracted from the Justice catalog!

Our kids spend so much time at the center of our own world that we can't blame them for assuming they're the center of the entire universe. But they're not—and it's good for our kids (as well as for the planet) to teach them this fact while they're still young. So don't be afraid to consider something greater than your kid's desires when making decisions—and to let her know you're doing so. "I hear you want to use new paper, but that would be wasteful. This paper has printing on one side, but it's perfectly clean on the other, and that's really all you need for doodling." "I know this sweater fell on the floor of your closet, but that doesn't mean it's dirty. It's wasteful to wash clothes that are still clean, so please hang it back up." "I see Mia has a new backpack, but your backpack is in great shape. It would be wasteful to buy you a new backpack when you don't need one." I'm not saying your kid will be thrilled to hear you say no—but she will be intrigued by your reasoning and may even get on board if you take the time to explore issues of wastefulness and conservation with her. It's pretty astounding to see, for example, how much water is wasted by running the washing machine unnecessarily and the impact of wasted water on the planet—and it's much more appealing to have this conversation with your kid than just nagging her to pick up her clothes.

And though you may fret about irreparably damaging your kid's self-worth by explaining that her wants do not actually outweigh what's best for planet Earth, learning to be less wasteful is really very empowering for your kid. I realize that she seems totally comfortable in her role as the ruler of your home—but she's not quite as secure as she seems. She's doing a lot of struggling with her place in her family, in her school, in her friendships, and yes, in the universe. Teaching her that her choices make a lasting impact, that she can influence the world around her, that she has a responsibility to—and a role in—something bigger than herself is a great gift for your kid. And while she may not thank you for reminding her to turn off the lights when she leaves a room, to put the empty bottle of Gatorade she scarfed after tennis in the recycling bin instead of leaving it on the couch, and to please get out of the shower before she drains the Atlantic, she will like being reminded that she matters in the world—and that she has a part to play.

Cutting down on waste is also a fantastic opportunity for family bonding, and honestly at this point in your kid's life, you need to grab as many of these as you possibly can. Encourage conservation as a shared value and a joint activity; "going green" is a cool enough concept these days that you won't completely mortify your kid by embracing it, and reminding each other to unplug appliances, close the refrigerator door, and throw on a sweater (hey, maybe the one that's still lying on the floor!) rather than crank up the heat another couple of degrees can actually be fun. You can even make it a friendly competition and reward the least wasteful person of the week by letting him or her choose a restaurant to try or a new movie to watch. And who knows—maybe these actions will resonate outside your house: If your kid's school is anything like mine, your kid probably comes home with regular doom-and-gloom reports about how we're destroying the planet—but fails to make the connection between this alarming news and the fact that she never remembers to turn her closet light off, like, I mean, ever. Your family's antiwaste campaign will underscore what your kid is learning and could even inspire her classmates to step up themselves.

And while I have your attention, please indulge me in one more rant—this one about the gigantic amount of food your kid may be wasting. Can I tell you that I had lunch at my kid's school recently and witnessed a pal get ready to throw away an entire serving of carrots? My kid, whom we've pretty thoroughly indoctrinated on this antiwaste thing and who will probably lose friends over it as the years drag on, asked what was wrong with the food. "Oh, look," the friend said, sighing, "this one carrot has a weird brown spot." "A weird brown spot?" my kid repeated incredulously. "Can't you just cut it off?" "I guess," the friend responded. "But I don't feel like it." My kid's attempt to liberate the carrots was stymied by the school's no-food-sharing policy, so into the garbage they went; after another year or two, I may have my kid motivated enough to dive into the trash can after them, but for now the story ends here.

While I hope your kid is not in the business of throwing away entire servings of vegetables, she is probably in the business of wasting food pretty regularly. I am not recommending that we return to the days of "clean your plate" or "think of children starving in

Africa"—but I am suggesting that routinely grabbing three slices of pizza but eating only two; abandoning a giant bowl of cereal after five spoonfuls; or being told, "It's okay, you don't have to finish that; just throw away what you don't want," rather than, "Stick the rest of that in the fridge, and you can eat it later," is not helping the world, nor is it helping your kid. If your kid takes food and doesn't finish it, or raises objections to the almost-perfectly-good snack you've just placed in front of her, don't force her to eat it—but don't noncommittally get rid of it or immediately replace it with something more appealing to her delicate taste buds, either. Making do with a damaged carrot is a pretty good life lesson, if you think about it—as is learning how to handle a knife (be careful, honey!) if your kid insists the weird brown spot be removed.

YOUR KID IS DEMANDING A GIGANTIC BIRTHDAY PARTY

◆ ◆ ◆ ◆ ◆ ◆ ◆ ◆

Did you know that when I turned seven, I had my birthday party at McDonald's? Please blink away your tears and keep your sympathetic pats to yourself—the party location was actually my choice, and except for Bradley Gordon throwing up in the parking lot, it was a totally awesome time. I even have a Kodak Instant Camera shot of my friends and me, arms around one another and mouths crammed with fries, and I swear to you we are really and truly smiling.

I know! How is this possible? McDonald's is a place you pass and shake your head at, a symbol of everything wrong with the world today. Your kid would never attend a birthday party at McDonald's, and if you even thought about hosting one—well, say good-bye to your tenuous membership in that fabulous circle of gorgeously coiffed moms, the ones I'm sure are really as nice as you say, except maybe they're not. You know that your kid deserves a million times better for her birthday, and she knows it, too, and you know she knows because she's been telling you for, like, the past three months exactly how she expects to mark her special day.

And therein lies the problem. Because, yes, a bash at McDonald's is way off the spectrum of possibilities, but so perhaps is the high-three-figure gala celebration your kid is picturing. Visions of facials and makeovers, multicourse fondue dinners, spa nights, and outings to concerts and amusement parks are dancing in her head—and while you may be dreading planning and shelling out for the big event, you feel compelled to do so in light of the fact that these are just the sorts of festivities your kid's been participating in all year long.

A birthday party's not just a birthday party anymore. It's a statement—about your kid, sure, but also about you and what league you want to play in. Your kid's been wined (hopefully not literally) and dined by her friends and their families for months, and her approaching birthday means it's time for you to step up. Not only does your kid want to be queen for a day among her peers, but you want to take your place as a mom to be reckoned with, one every bit as able to pull off a fabulous fete as the yummy mummies you've fallen in with. An Evite to the bowling alley is not going to cut it—not for your kid, sure, but also not for you.

I am not entirely without sympathy here. After receiving professionally printed invitations to the first birthday parties of my kid's fellow playgroupers (one was at a beautiful country club pool, though of course none of the guests could swim), I arranged for my own kid a circus-themed celebration featuring a custom cake, a certified early-childhood educator to lead enrichment games (don't even ask), and elaborate goody bags that mostly ended up trampled on the floor. I told you he was turning one, right? Nor did I learn my lesson that year; later birthday revelries included a "nature lovers" gathering for which I handwrote invitations onto large dried leaves (did you know leaves can actually be stamped and sent through the mail?), a moon-time pajama party complete with moon bounce (for twenty prekindergarteners—do not try this at home), and an "old-fashioned" celebration for which I hired two assistants and invested untold hours of cleaning in order to achieve the perfect laid-back, casual atmosphere such a shindig required. The assistants were also conscripted into toweling off fifteen soaking wet children as a sudden thunderstorm interrupted their "old-fashioned" outdoor play and sent them scurrying into my heretofore immaculate home.

It was not until my kid turned seven that I had the revelation I will share with you now: It was all for shit. All my efforts, all my anxiety, all my determination to host the perfect birthday party—they benefited exactly no one, including my kid and me. As it turns out, a custom birthday cake tastes no better than one you pick up at the grocery store, or bake yourself if that's your thing; invitations you slave away on are no more effective than an Evite you send out between meetings; and the party games run by paid professionals are no more engaging than those your guests will come up with if tossed outside and left to their own devices. Oh, and the moms who will judge you for any of these things—or who will enter your home and not-so-sweetly ask if that living room set is from your grad school days and when do you plan to replace it—are not the moms you want to be hanging out with, anyway.

How do I know this is true? Because as my kid's seventh birthday approached, the idea of planning a party so exhausted me that

I decided not to try anymore. I asked my kid what his favorite thing to do with his friends was; he responded, "play soccer"; and I e-mailed his friends' parents with an invitation to join us at a local park for soccer and cake. It was a totally fun event, especially for me, as facilitating a boys' soccer game was right up my husband's alley and left me free to sip Diet Dr Pepper in the shade while vaguely "keeping an eye on things." And while I worried that some parents might see our party as cheap, and while they probably did, most of them seemed plenty happy, anyway—especially because the party's cheapness allowed them to drop off older and younger siblings and enjoy a kid-free afternoon.

If you are willing to take my word on this, you will find that planning your kid's birthday party has just become a lot less stressful—and maybe even fun. Your kid is still young enough to want to please you as well as her peers; so she'll actually listen and consider if you respond to her over-the-top ideas with a friendly "That sounds fun, and I know how much you liked doing that at Emmery's party. But let's come up with something that's just about you." Then see where the conversation goes. It may turn out that your kid was feeling pressured to mount an extravagant celebration but would actually love to invite her pals to the bowling alley, to a favorite restaurant, or just to your house for a pajama-and-movie night; it may be that she'd be open to taking her one or two closest friends for a day trip or other special outing; it may be that some out-of-the-box but easy activities will capture her imagination and become the centerpiece of her big day. (Post–seventh birthday party highlights for my kids have included nighttime backyard treasure hunts with flashlights—the prizes were all from the dollar store, but the guests didn't care; covering the floor with Bubble Wrap and dancing around; and squirting Purell on our granite countertop and lighting it on fire—it's amazingly cool, I'm serious.) Even if your kid remains fixated on pedicures or fondue, you can still shift the location from a four-star salon or restaurant to your house and hire a couple of teenagers to help out so you don't spend the afternoon washing her friends' feet (I mean, yuck).

And while your kid's birthday party should be a (reasonable) celebration of her and everything that makes her special, it's also a great chance to teach her consideration and kindness. If you would prefer that your kid not grow up to judge potential friends by the condition of their couches (yes, it was from grad school, and yes, we did buy it used, okay?), the time to start is now. This means balancing your kid's desire to control her guest list with respect for how the people who don't make the cut might feel; you need not invite her whole grade, of course, but you also can't invite her whole grade minus three people. And if your kid's primary clique has six members but she really likes only four of them—well, now is not the time to let the hanger-on know. And I am sure you already realize this, but don't forget to tell your kid: Unless every single child in the school has been invited, talking about her upcoming bash in the cafeteria, on the playground, or in class is, like, the hugest no. And if she's promising to be totally discreet in handing out invitations at school, and "no one who's not invited will know because I'm just going to slide them into people's lockers, and, Mom, it's totally fine, and Emmery's mom let *her*"—don't let her.

Not to sound too horribly sappy, which if you've read this far you know I absolutely am not; but once you make your kid's birthday less about social positioning and more about your actual kid, you'll be happily surprised at how meaningful and special the occasion becomes. And you can deepen its significance by refocusing attention—yours and your kid's—on how this occasion fits into the bigger picture of her life and family: Why not break up the party planning by telling stories about your kid's earliest days, looking at baby photos and old videos, and sharing family heirlooms and legends that recall the person for whom she was named, or great-grandparents she never knew? You might even consider making your kid's birthday an opportunity for her to help others; very few kids are up for an "in lieu of gifts, please donate to charity" tagline on their invitations, and I certainly do not suggest you cajole/shame/force your present-craving kid into joining their ranks, but surely your kid would enjoy receiving a Kiva Card or small check to be donated to a cause of her choice.

And speaking of presents: Did you know that in certain cultures—or at least on eBay—special gifts are recommended for the mother of the birthday child? If not stuffing thirty goody bags full of crap, or not scrubbing your floor in preparation for the arrival of a horde of second graders, feels inadequate to the momentousness of the occasion—feel free to follow up your kid's birthday party by giving a gift to yourself. Unless you are the patient and understanding soul who married Bradley Gordon, I suggest a very large order of McDonald's fries.

YOUR KID IS A TERRIBLE TRAVELER

◆ ◆ ◆ ◆ ◆ ◆ ◆ ◆

A family vacation sounds so idyllic, until you realize that the people accompanying you on this adventure are, in fact, the same family you have at home. The disappointing revelations continue as your kid evinces no more enthusiasm for packing his own suitcase than he does for locating his arm pads before lacrosse practice, and eagerly points out as many shortcomings in your out-of-town accommodations as he does at the old homestead (yes, the tile in the hotel bathroom is cracked, and yes, we're all aware that Jonah's house has a fire pit and a trampoline). By day three (two? one?), you are wondering how many massages it will take to get you over this getaway, and not-entirely-just-for-fun Googling "adults-only resort properties," while your scowling kid helps himself to another waffle at the breakfast buffet (all part of the meal plan!) and demands to know if he is going to have any fun today.

Okay. Let's rewind and try this whole thing again.

It is actually possible to take a fantastic family trip—and if you are lucky enough to have the time and the resources to travel with your kid, you totally should. However, you should read this first.

Before you do anything—anything!—repeat these words to yourself: "I am the parent, and I get to decide." Yes, I'm talking to you—say it! Say it over and over, forcing conviction and confidence into your voice, until you really, honestly believe these words and are prepared to act accordingly. Why? Because these words are the secret to your success. Along with fuzzy slippers from home and a white-noise app on your smartphone, they are your greatest tool in ensuring a genuinely enjoyable family vacation—a vacation in which you get to be an active and happy participant rather than a cranky chaperon, a faux-cheerful camp counselor, or an overworked, unappreciated tour guide.

Because here is secret-to-success number two: You deserve a vacation, too. Somewhere along the line, "family vacation" became synonymous with "going someplace your kid wants to go," and that, my friend, is just wrong. If you are flexible and would like to include your kid in some aspects of planning the vacation, that is great—you will make him feel like a part of the process, convey the sense that you are in this together, and get all of you excited about sharing an adventure. However, limits need to be placed on your kid's inclusion. For example: There is absolutely no reason in the world to begin the trip-planning process by excitedly telling your kid that a vacation is in the works, asking him where he'd like to go—and then feeling bound by whatever he says, lest you disappoint him or spoil his fun or something equally ridiculous. You are the parent, and you get to decide.

Now, I am not suggesting that you schlep your kid on a five-day biking tour exploring the wonders of the Italian countryside (I'll come, though), but neither should you dismiss as selfish your desire for a getaway that includes at least a few adult elements—maybe some pretty scenery, maybe some intellectual enrichment, maybe some physical activity, maybe some great shopping, maybe a bit of pampering, whatever floats your boat. Your kid can not only survive but actually enjoy a trip that has not been arranged around his every preference—and a couple of museum outings or a few hours in the kids' club while you relax with a pedicure and massage are a small price for your kid to pay in order to have Happy Mom rather than Stressed Mom as his travel companion.

Yes, Disney people, I hear you. I realize that there are many parents out there who honestly, truly, deeply want to spend their free time at Disney, and who find fulfillment, joy, and happiness in vacations at theme parks, family beach resorts, and the like. If this is you, that is awesome, and I can't wait to see the photo book of your kid rocking a set of Mickey ears and riding the Seven Dwarfs Mine Train. But if this is not you, please don't pretend that it is. It's not fair to you—obviously!—but it's also not fair to your kid. You will be able to sustain your chirpy facade for only a (very) limited time; and the second your kid gets a little whiny, fails to display the requisite amount of gratitude for the churro you just paid, like, a million dollars for, or complains that the line for a ride is too long, that facade will come crashing down. You will suddenly morph from Bubbly, Exuberant Mom to Maleficent Mom; and the ensuing fireworks (not the fun kind) and ruined day will not be your kid's fault but your own. It is far better to know and honor your own personality and limits, even if it means your kid ages out of childhood without a trip to the Magic Kingdom, than to pretend to be someone you're not. Which is actually pretty good advice in general if you want to go write it down. I'll wait.

Of course, choosing your destination is only the beginning. There is still the not-inconsiderable matter of packing up the shit you'll need, a task that is not only a complete pain in the ass but also far above your kid's skill set—so by all means, have your kid veg out in front of *Dog with a Blog* while you take care of it for him. Wait, wait, I'm kidding! Seriously, turn off the TV and work with your kid to create a packing list. Talk with him about how long you'll be away, what activities you'll be doing, what the weather will be like; and help him figure out what outfits he'll want, if he needs a jacket, that kind of stuff. Yes, he might get annoyed or wish you'd just take care of packing for him—but if you approach him as a partner in the trip and really let him make some decisions for himself, he might also surprise you by jumping on board and taking some responsibility. And unless you are traveling through freezing weather and are less than ninety-five percent sure your kid will remember to pack the COAT you wrote in huge letters and underlined twice, consider not checking his bag to be sure he followed the list perfectly—wearing mismatched socks every day or having to wash out his undies every night in the hotel bathtub because he thought two pairs would see him through a six-day vacation is not only a learning experience but also stuff you and your kid will one day recall as a highlight of your travels together.

And speaking of together, please remember that your kid is no longer a helpless infant who requires eighty pounds of equipment for every outing—and, by the way, the person carting that equipment around is you—but is a growing and able-bodied person more than capable of doing a little schlepping of his own. Have you seen those kids pulling small wheeled suitcases through airports while their parents—weighed down with the massive bags of stuff those kids will actually be wearing, using, and misplacing throughout the trip—gasp for air and praise them as "helpers"? Of course you have; they're everywhere. But have you seen the three kids dragging humongous duffels through the airport and only occasionally wondering aloud why Mom is carrying nothing more than her laptop and backpack? Those are mine, and they are awesome. I highly recommend you initiate this practice in your own family travels; and, by the way, a handy response is, "After all the years I carried your suitcases, you must be so happy to be able to do your part," or "We're all working together to make this trip great, and this is a way for you to contribute." Let me know if your kid greets these answers with understanding nods and renewed enthusiasm for the task; mine do not, but they do keep dragging the bags, which is good enough for me.

What used to be the most challenging/miserable (choose your adjective!) part of traveling has, of course, been rendered completely innocuous with the advances of technology. A kid who ten years ago would need a pack of Bendaroos, five toy cars, two jars of playdough, finger puppets, Color Wonder markers, and a thousand increasingly impassioned reminders to Please! Be! Quiet! in order to make it through a three-hour flight or drive can now quite serenely travel from New York to New Zealand, as long as the tablet battery or the in-flight entertainment system holds out. But while I am all for a peaceful, happy journey, I do want to put in a brief plug for unplugging, at least part of the time.

Yes, flights and car trips are a great time to zone out on games and movies—but they are also a great time to bond by reading a new book aloud; playing goofy games like I Spy, Geography, or Twenty Questions; looking for the states on license plates on passing cars or the letters of the alphabet on signs and buildings; marveling over the crazy shit for sale in the SkyMall catalog; or just daydreaming, chilling out, and talking about the coming trip. Yes, you miss a lot of angst by securing a handheld device or a DVD player for each kid—but you also miss some potentially very nice moments. (And if you like the idea of unplugging during part of a long car trip but your kids are too cranky and ootsy for sweet-family-bonding-type activities, consider more subversive options like crushing stuff in the automatic window, looking for the most inappropriate billboard, and—this last one is from my friend Heather—it's too horrible for me to contemplate but maybe you'll like it—Roadkill Bingo, which is played exactly as you are imagining.)

And when you finally arrive at your destination, welcome! I have no idea where you are (and if you're in the Italian countryside, that pisses me off, because I totally would have come) so I am not going to offer a day-by-day guide to getting the most out of your vacation. However, I am going to offer one final recommendation:

Assume that things are going to go wrong, and that it is okay. There is really no such thing as a perfect vacation—and if you pressure yourself to have one, you are going to be too stressed and miserable to enjoy what is probably a very nice getaway. Don't beat yourself up if you feel cranky one day, don't feel guilty for taking your kid on an outing when he's made it quite clear he'd rather sit in the hotel room with your phone, and don't freak out if the beach is closed one morning due to shark sightings (well, maybe then). You have no idea how these setbacks will play out, or how they will be remembered by your kid.

I will share that the most horrible trip our family ever took was to New Orleans, which I understand is a very nice city that you should definitely visit, but perhaps not with young children during March Madness in a Bourbon Street–area hotel. Anyway, for all the complaining, whining, and grumbling I heard from my kids that weekend, the experience has become one of our most cherished memories. "Remember how we thought that guy lying in the street in front of our hotel was dead?" my son will ask. "And then he finally got up and started drinking again? That was amazing." So really, you never know.

YOUR KID WON'T TAKE NO FOR AN ANSWER

◆ ◆ ◆ ◆ ◆ ◆ ◆ ◆

I have some bad news for you. You are probably sitting down already, unless you are standing up reading this in a bookstore, in which case you should buy the book, then sit down. You ready? Okay.

Your kid is not going to grow up to argue cases before the Supreme Court.

I realize this news comes as a blow, especially arriving so soon after recent performances at ball games and violin recitals have clarified that careers in sports and entertainment may be out of reach as well. But we both know that the dismay and alarm that accompany the end of this particular dream are about more than wanting your kid to achieve amazing things or to understand the majesty of law or to eventually obtain a remunerative job so you will not be forced to continue paying him to feed the cat and occasionally pick up his room. We both know you had something else—something even more significant—riding on the image of your kid becoming a top-notch attorney.

It explained so much, right? Because your kid is clearly blossoming as a tireless and effective litigator. He's prodigiously able to tease out the inconsistencies and unfairness in every single thing you do or say, even while simultaneously playing on his Xbox or scarfing a roll of Girl Scout cookies. And his dedication to pointing out these discrepancies, and his creativity in interpreting them to his own advantage—well, it's really a thing of beauty. The crowning glory, of course, is his doggedness in holding fast to his convictions and his commitment to do whatever it takes—for however long it takes—to make you see the situation the same way.

Yep, these are awesome qualities for a future star attorney. The problem is, your kid is not the only one who's developed them. These talents are shared by millions of kids, each of them a recently minted expert in finding loopholes in orders issued by parents; crafting earnest and lengthy explanations of how a parent is being mean or unjust; and employing a combination of logical reasoning, force of will, and general disrespectfulness to get their own way. And while you may imagine the glimmerings of greatness in your particular kid, it's time to accept the unfortunate fact that he's just another face in the crowd—and that the rest of the world sees not a crop of young defenders of civil rights but a bunch of ill-mannered children who refuse to take no for an answer.

Let's be honest: That's what your kid's forays into law come down to, isn't it? He's not lobbying on behalf of the poor and the marginalized—he's lobbying on behalf of himself. He wants to eat a Hot Pocket for dinner, he wants an extra half hour of screen time, he wants you to take him to Colin's house right now even though he hasn't cleaned up his closet like he was supposed to over the weekend, he wants to stay up later, he wants to see a PG-13 movie, he wants to go out for cocktails with girlfriends on a school/work night (wait, that was me). These are not the concerns of a budding idealist committed to justice and clean air and universal health care—they are simply the concerns of a kid who wants his own way and who will run roughshod over everyone until he gets it.

Consider the following: Your kid's just brought home a science test. The grade's not terrible, but neither is it particularly good, and you're sure he could have done better, especially in light of the fact that he spent the evening before the test shooting hoops in the driveway and informing you that he didn't need to study because Colin wasn't, and anyway it was going to be soooo easy. You've been careful to react in exactly the right way—sharing your disappointment without unduly pressuring him, letting him own the grade while expressing support, giving him space to fail but encouraging him to succeed, blah blah blah. Anyway, you've wrapped up the whole conversation by announcing that he'll have to forgo his nightly allotment of Disney XD in favor of correcting the test.

It's at this point that things get lively. The gears spin as your kid sits up straighter, purses his lips, and begins looking for the way out. "Can I correct the test and then watch?"

"No, sweetie. You can't watch tonight."

"But why not? I mean, if I correct the test and have time after."

"Well, because . . . it's a good lesson to miss your shows when you haven't done your best."

"What? I did so do my best. The test was just really hard."

"Well, then, you should have studied instead of playing basketball." (Said a trifle smugly. You've got him!)

Or maybe not. "I didn't know the stuff about the digestive system would be on the test! Remember I missed that day because you took me to the dentist?"

"Yes, I remember, but . . ."

"And Colin said it wouldn't be on the test, so I didn't study it. But I know it now, and I can correct the test in, like, ten minutes."

"I hear you, but . . ."

"And my show doesn't start for twenty minutes, and I finished my other homework. Are you going to let Josh watch without me?"

"I hadn't thought about it, but, yes, I guess . . ."

"Because that's really not fair, because he's only in first grade. He's too young to have to study. If he gets to watch, I definitely should."

"But, sweetie, you didn't study for the test."

"I know, and I'm really sorry. But look, I'm doing the corrections now. Oh my gosh, this is so easy. I'll be done in ten minutes, so I'll definitely be able to watch. Okay?"

"Um, well . . ."

"Thanks, Mom! You always understand me."

This is how it's gone every time, right? Your kid exposes the flaws in your logic, dismantles your explanations and defenses, and leaves you wondering why you thought your initial idea even made sense in the first place. After all, you're committed to treating your kid fairly, respectfully, consistently, and justly—so how could you possibly stick to your original course of action once he's demonstrated how utterly lacking it was in these important qualities? And as for that niggling sense of irritation and suspicion that you've been had—well, you better tamp that down quickly. Would you really rather be raising a kid who blindly accepts authority and doesn't know how to stand up for himself?

Actually, in this particular case, maybe you would. Because while you're taking the broad view of the situation—preoccupying yourself with issues like fairness, respect, consistency, and justice—your kid is preoccupied only with worming his way out of a situation he doesn't like. And, not to make you feel like an idiot, but he's totally taking advantage of your ideals.

People, please. Respecting your kid's viewpoint and treating him equitably is superimportant, yes—but it's not the only superimportant thing in the world, and it becomes far less important the minute your kid starts refusing to take no for an answer. If your kid is constantly mustering arguments against your reasonable expectations and discipline, it's no longer time to worry about being scrupulously consistent and fair. Instead, it's time to start worrying about being firm and authoritative.

And it's time to get reacquainted with the phrase "because I said so."

I sense you've just backed away in horror, but please come back. Then go back in time and remember how much you hated hearing an adult say "because I said so." Then remember exactly why you hated hearing it.

It effectively ended the conversation, right? It signaled that the discussion was closed. It meant that your carefully crafted claims and arguments and protests would go unspoken. It showed that the adult was in charge and had made the decision and you couldn't do anything about it.

Now return to daily life with your kid, and imagine yourself not as the speakee but as the speaker. Doesn't "because I said so" suddenly seem kind of nice?

It totally is. Because as important as it is for you to listen to your kid, to hear out his legitimate complaints, to empower him to stand up for himself, it's also important to clarify just who is in charge here (you) and what his obligations to you include (listening respectfully and doing what you say). It's difficult to accomplish this when your kid regards your telling him to do something as the opening salvo in a long and complicated negotiation, and when you're tying yourself in knots attempting to justify basic parenting decisions to a nine-year-old. This is where "because I said so"—stated firmly, accompanied by a brief smile, and followed by body language indicating that you are so done talking about this—comes in.

Believe it or not, "because I said so" is as good for your kid as it is for you. Because while he may seem to enjoy refusing to take no for an answer and wearing you down until he gets his way, your kid is actually kind of freaked out at how easily you succumb to his manipulations. Yes, he wants to be heard; yes, he wants to win the occasional battle; yes, he wants to know that you respect him and his desires—but he also wants to feel assured of your leadership and competence, and to trust that you know what's best for him. The easy confidence and calm certainty conveyed by a properly delivered "because I said so" are actually great gifts for your kid.

And don't even tell me that accepting "because I said so" and learning to take no for an answer will turn your kid into an unthinking automaton ready to knuckle under to the authority of any adult who comes along. I mean, ha. Have you not met your child? It will take a lot more than that to break his spirit! A fact which may prove comforting or depressing, depending on the day.

SECTION 3

Your Bratty Tween—Ages Nine Through Twelve

INTRODUCING YOUR BRATTY TWEEN

◆ ◆ ◆ ◆ ◆ ◆ ◆ ◆

As if you hadn't already paid your dues by schlepping your kid through his years as a budding brat and a bratty child, now you're saddled with a bratty tween. Whether you call it middle childhood, preadolescence, or a shit storm, you and your kid are entering a period of major changes that include increasing dependence on peers, growing independence from you and the rest of the family, and emotional highs and lows that will regularly suck both of you dry. In addition to hanging on to some old and perhaps-not-fully-resolved bratty behaviors, your kid will now prove to be a fountain of rudeness to loved ones, completely disinterested in assisting around the house, and ambivalent about being involved with you in any meaningful way, especially if it's in public or there might possibly be someone he knows in a thirty-mile radius. He may also curse a lot.

Yes, your kid is exasperating and exhausting; and yes, it's totally understandable that his every outburst of brattiness will provoke an equal and opposite reaction from you. (Yay for Isaac Newton—who knew he was such a parenting guru?) But the key to surviving—and maybe even enjoying, I'm serious—these years with your bratty tween is to do a lot less reacting and a lot more listening, absorbing, and engaging. Sometimes your kid's obnoxiousness is really a plea for understanding, and sometimes his most outrageous and repulsive antics are attempts to get your attention, and sometimes his withdrawal from you and the family pains him even more than it does the rest of you. If you can stanch your impulse to answer his brattiness with anger, to match his insensitivity and sarcasm with a few cutting witticisms of your own, or to get far, far away every time he's in a mood, you will do your kid and yourself a big favor—and both of you may find these tween years to be, well, if not the greatest time of your life together, at least not the worst.

Does this all mean that you give your kid a pass when he rolls his eyes at you for daring to suggest that he put down his phone long enough to set the table, that he be permitted to let fly streams of "shit" and "fuck" when he can't find his hockey stick (check the front hallway!), or that you fix your kid's snack every day because he works so hard at school and deserves to come home and relax? Of course not—really, have I taught you nothing so far? Parenting your tween is a complicated mixture of enforcing limits and being accommodating, asserting authority and inviting discussion, understanding why your kid wants you to say yes but still saying no, and yearning to glue yourself to your kid because you fear he can't make it otherwise but backing off and watching him succeed (or sometimes fail) without you. Most of all, though, it's about remembering that underneath this challenging, annoying, frustrating creature lies an absolutely wonderful kid, and ending the bratty behavior that keeps people—even you, and maybe even himself—from seeing who he really is.

Well, that really clears things up, doesn't it? Ha! But don't worry; the next fourteen chapters will explain how to put these grand themes into practice when your kid ignores your birthday or demands a pair of running shoes that cost more than your favorite dress or slips outside with Purell, a match, and the announcement that he's going to do a science experiment in the front yard (true story!). Chock-full of real-life examples, sample statements to use on your kid, hints at the bigger issues your kid's behavior may be illuminating, and my generally telling you what to do all the time, this section will totally get you through the next few years with your bratty tween. I almost promise.

YOUR KID NEEDS TO TAKE RESPONSIBILITY

◆ ◆ ◆ ◆ ◆ ◆ ◆ ◆

It's, like, eleven o'clock at night, and you have a million things you'd rather be doing—including sleeping—but your kid needs a lunch for school tomorrow. You grill a Gruyère-and-sliced-apple sandwich (it looked better on Pinterest, but what can you do?), bag celery sticks and ranch, chill a box of organic vanilla milk, and add a fun-size Milky Way, just to be nice. You arrange everything in your kid's insulated bento box, and the next afternoon—as you settle down to reheated leftovers—happily envision your tween savoring the fruits of your late-night labor.

So it totally sucks to have your kid come home with three-quarters of the sandwich untouched, the bag of celery unopened—and a litany of complaints. You're only somewhat comforted to learn you're not alone in your ineptitude—apparently not a single one of your kid's friends' moms packs a decent lunch.

Of course your kid should treat your efforts with more gratitude; of course you feel hurt and angry and unappreciated. May I suggest, however, that instead of reacting to your kid's moaning with wrath, defensiveness, or—worst—apologies, you treat her grievances as a gift: Clearly the time has arrived for your kid to start making her own lunch.

Why am I making such a big deal about lunch? In part because packing kids' lunches is a complete pain in the ass—I have about a million friends, and maybe three have never complained about this task—but mostly because handing lunch making off to your kid is the first step of an essential stage in her development. Even more important than saving you tons of time, even more important than eliminating the hassle of cleaning that bento box, even more important than being able to eat the last leftover slice of gluten-free pizza at midnight rather than sliding it into your kid's lunch for almost certain rejection the following day—having your kid pack her own lunch introduces her to the art of being responsible for herself.

I can see you dancing a jig at the prospect of never assembling another turkey BLT for your kid, only to hear that Stella's mom packs her a cookie butter sandwich, like, every day—and, honestly, this is only the beginning. Here are some lunch-related tips, along with a blueprint to help you hand over the reins of responsibility in lots of other areas—and explanations of why you should.

Let's do lunch. Be cheerful when announcing your kid's new role as lunch maker, dismissing her protestations of incompetence with "I know you can do it!" and the reminder that at her age, you were cooking dinner for your entire family (I'm willing to believe this is the truth unless you tell me otherwise). Explain the principles of a balanced meal, promise (threaten?) occasional checks to ensure that she's not pilfering your Diet Dr Pepper, and be certain that her lunch is packed before she goes to bed at night. (I can tell you from painful experience that if your kid waits until morning to prepare the lunch, you'll end up doing it yourself while she endlessly brushes her hair.)

Don't lose focus when your kid whines that she's the only person in the entire school who makes her own lunch. Acknowledge that this is probably true, but add that it also means she is the only person in the entire school whose parents recognize her competence and trust her to take responsibility for her own meal. She may grumble and give you the eye roll, but she will also remember—and appreciate—being called competent and trustworthy. (Anyway, she won't be the only lunch maker for long; soon enough, your friends will find out about your new technique and decide to implement it themselves.) And definitely don't waste time wondering if making your kid's lunch is proof that you love her. It is not. My kid makes his own lunch and I love him so much that I'm paying for his orthodontia. I'd rather make his lunch and have him pay for the orthodontia, but so it goes.

Teach your kid to be ready on time. How many times do you remind your kid to get ready for gymnastics, and how many times do you raise your voice as she refuses to stop posting photos of her new leotard on Instagram and actually put the thing on? How many times have you sped/fumed across town because she couldn't decide what to wear to a friend's birthday party and is now running hugely late? How would you like for your answer to go from "zillions" to "zero"? It totally can—again, it's just a matter of handing over responsibility to your kid.

Explain that from now on, you are not going to nag your kid to hurry up, watch the clock, etc.—you are just going to remind her what plans she's made and let her handle it from there. If your kid fulfills her responsibility by being ready on time, do your part by cheerfully (even if you don't feel glad about yet another drive to annoying Lexi's house) taking her where she needs to go. If, however, your kid goofs around and announces at 3:53 that she's ready for her 4:00 cheer class, and can you drive extra fast because the gym is twenty minutes away, your answer turns to no. Yes, your kid will react with fury—but stand strong, because you are succeeding in handing over yet another responsibility to your tween. You are also succeeding in striking "frantic drives across town" from future to-do lists—because your kid will never run so late again.

Consider that your kid's teacher may not be a complete idiot out to get your child. Did you know that in the old days—like when we were in school—a parent did not automatically take a kid's word over that of the teacher? Of course, that was because teachers were better then, and your kid's teacher in particular clearly hates your kid—but hmmm. What if your kid's teacher is right when he suggests that your kid is not reaching her potential and that she might have done better on her end-of-semester project had she and Lexi not spent much of their in-class work time whispering about *The Bachelorette*? Rather than springing into Mama Bear mode and charging into your kid's classroom to defend her against any perceived maltreatment, try taking a deep breath and assuming that her teacher is on to something—and that it's up to your kid to set things right.

Guiding your kid to be aware of the impression she makes, the fact that others are entitled to their own points of view, and her obligation to get along with people who may not find her perfect and precious in every way will help her understand how conflicts might develop between her and those in authority—and will also give her some tools to handle these issues without resorting to defensiveness and a plea for her Mama Bear to step in. Of course your kid may occasionally find herself in tough situations she can't manage on her own—but taking responsibility for those she can will build her skills, confidence, and maturity, which is what these tween years are all about.

Don't listen when your kid's bullshitting you. This seriously happened to a cousin of mine: His daughter Ava was spending the afternoon on her pal's boat (nice, yeah, I know), and the girls decided to go swimming in the bay. The pal had a turquoise bikini body chain, which sounds maybe not superappropriate for a twelve-year-old girl but they didn't ask me, and Ava did say it was cute, so who knows. Anyway, the girl jumped into the water, then realized she had left her body chain on the boat. "Toss it to me!" she yelled to Ava. "Uh, are you sure?" Ava responded. "Yes!" she called impatiently. "I want it now. Toss it!" Ava did, and you can guess what happened—the girl didn't catch the chain, and down it sank into the ocean, lost forever.

What you may not guess (but maybe you would) is what happened next: The girl started screaming that Ava had thrown her body chain in the ocean, and she rallied her parents to reprimand Ava and demand she buy a replacement. It never occurred to the parents to wonder why Ava—a heretofore sweet and responsible friend—would essentially destroy their daughter's property, or to question the holes in their daughter's story. Nor did it occur to Body Chain Girl to examine her own role in the situation or to do anything besides cast blame and get a new chain ASAP. Nor will any of this ludicrousness and drama befall you if you find the courage to call your kid on her bullshit and to teach her not only to accept praise and credit for her good choices—but also to take responsibility when she does something careless or wrong.

Do listen when your kid's telling you something important. Say your kid has adapted to this new approach and is (mostly) handling her responsibilities. Then say a few days go by when she's running late for cheer or refusing to make her lunch or similar. Rather than assuming she's regressed and fallen back to her old ways, consider that she's trying to tell you something. For example: One of my friends got so sick of nagging her kid to get ready for soccer that she finally announced she was just not going to take him anymore; her kid shocked her by responding with tears of relief. The kid had long before stopped enjoying soccer but feared his parents' reaction if he let them know he wanted to quit the team.

Once your kid starts taking responsibility for her needs and activities, she earns the right to be treated differently—not as a fully responsible adult, but not as an irresponsible or flighty child, either. React thoughtfully and patiently to lapses in her behavior, and listen to her ideas about changes she might like to make, new goals she might like to pursue, new ways she might like to do things. One of the privileges of taking responsibility for yourself is having that self heard—make sure you extend that privilege to your kid.

If all this sounds totally amazing, get going and get excited—but maybe not too excited. Remember that even the most responsible version of your tween is still, well, your tween—the same one who not all that long ago was defending *The Bachelorette* as a subject worthy of classroom discussion time. Although I am actually willing to entertain her arguments on that one, especially if she makes me a Gruyère-and-sliced-apple sandwich and promises never to wear a bikini body chain, like, ever.

YOUR KID SASSES YOU

◆ ◆ ◆ ◆ ◆ ◆ ◆ ◆

Here are some things I have heard kids say to their parents:

> "Mom! That's so stupid!"
>
> "*Please*, Mom, just stay away from my friends."
>
> "Dad, that shirt makes you look really fat."
>
> "Anabeth's mom's hair is so much nicer than yours."

And here are some things I have heard kids say to other kids in front of their parents:

> "I can't believe my mom won't let you come over, Amelia. That sucks. She is soooo mean."
>
> "Don't even worry about it"—"it" being the instruction just issued by a parent to please stop eating the dessert intended as an after-dinner treat—"you can totally take another cookie."

"I can't believe she's not letting us get soda. That's so dumb."

"My dad does that all the time. He's crazy embarrassing."

And here are some things I have heard the parents say to their kids:

"Well, I guess I'm just an idiot, right?"

"Sweetheart, please don't say that, okay? It hurts my feelings."

"Honey, I'm not trying to be mean. You just have to go to swimming this afternoon, remember? Maybe Amelia can come over next weekend."

(Nervous laughter) "Wow, you girls sure are enjoying those cookies!"

What the fuck is going on here? Why is your kid being such a sassy, mouthy brat—and why are you responding with self-deprecation and appeasement? Does your kid have an ax or something, and you are trying to get her to calm down and put it away? Or have you just grown so accustomed to having your kid speak to you this way that you no longer realize how hugely, seriously, incredibly messed up the dynamic between you has become?

I am going to bet on the latter (but if I am wrong, yes, please do whatever it takes to disarm your kid, and maybe you should not have an ax lying around in the first place)—which means that you need a significant pep talk and a reminder of the way things are supposed to go down between parent and child. Simply put, your kid is not supposed to be speaking to you this way.

Now, I realize that your kid has many friends and that you have heard all of them mouthing off to their parents on many, many occasions; and I, too, have watched all the television shows that depict sassy kids outsmarting the clueless grown-ups clogging up their homes and schools—so I totally understand that when your kid rolls her eyes every time you open your mouth, you might figure that it's just part of being a parent. But, oh my gosh, it's so not.

There are lots of phrases people use to describe the way your kid is behaving: She's "forging her own identity," or "struggling with separation," or "articulating her emotions." All these things are true; as a tween, your kid is realizing who she is, feeling alternately thrilled and terrified that it's not you, and exploring the full range of self-expression and assertiveness. Not only is this stage perfectly normal, it's also centrally important to her development and eventual independence. However, understanding what your kid is doing is not the same as giving her license to keep doing it.

People, please. Would you let some random adult call you stupid, then answer agreeably that, yeah, you must be a moron? Would you let casual acquaintances mock your car, then invite them to climb aboard for a trip to the mall with Kylie? Would you let your spouse tell you that you look horrible, then offer to make his or her favorite dinner and clean the toilet while he or she plays video games? If this sounds like an awesome life to you, you might actually rather be searching dominant-submissive erotica bestsellers on Kindle (updated hourly!) than reading this book—but if you prefer a more conventional existence, it's time to acknowledge that things between you and your kid need to change.

I know, I know: You can handle it. Sure, being mocked and abused by your kid hurts a little (okay, a lot)—but it's totally worth it in order to keep open the lines of communication between you. If you insist that your kid speak to you with consideration and courtesy—what if she just stops speaking to you entirely?

This is a legitimate concern, but it cannot be your only concern. Because as important as it is that your kid feel comfortable sharing her opinions and her convictions, it's also important that she learn to share them in an atmosphere of mutual respect and kindness. And although you've read in, like, a million books that you should make sure your kid feels she can tell you anything, that doesn't necessarily mean that she should be telling you your dress is the most hideous thing she's ever seen and that she'll die, seriously die, if you're wearing it when you pick her up from school. And last—but certainly not least—even though your kid seems very happy ridiculing every single thing you do, and scorning you in front of anyone and everyone she knows, a big part of her is freaking out—and desperately hoping you'll shut her up.

Here's the thing: Your kid might act like she totally can't stand you (and yeah, sometimes she can't, and sometimes it's mutual)—but at the same time, she's totally depending on you. You're her home base, her anchor, the safe place she's both rebelling against and counting on as a refuge whenever she needs it; and part of what she's doing by sassing you is testing how strong, how reliable, that refuge really is. Every time you let your kid insult you, every time you respond to her sass with weakness, self-effacement, or humility, you are failing her in a huge way. Instead of modeling self-respect, assertiveness, and confidence, you are modeling self-doubt, diffidence (look it up), and insecurity. Instead of showing your kid that you are her rock and her champion, you are showing her that you're ineffectual and uncertain. Instead of proving to your kid that she can count on you when things get rough—that you'd swim across an ocean and walk across a continent to protect her—you're demonstrating that you'll cave the minute an eleven-year-old says something mean. If you can't defend yourself against your kid's telling you you're an idiot, how is she supposed to trust you to defend her at all?

So for your kid's sake, and for your own, I offer these helpful guidelines:

ONE: If other people don't address you this way, neither should your kid. Words like "stupid," "idiot," and "dumb" are not okay; neither is theatrically rolled eyes or mocking you in front of her friends.

TWO: There is a boundary between expressing yourself and hurting others, and your kid needs to stay on the right side of it. "Mom, could you please not wear that dinosaur hat when you pick me up?" (actual quote!) is okay—"Mom, I can't believe you asked Isabella how her day was—you are so embarrassing. I seriously cannot stand it!" is not.

THREE: Tune in to yourself. You know how you feel when something bad is happening? Your heart races, you feel a little breathless, a sense of impending doom closes in—something along those lines, right? Have you ever noticed that you experience these sensations when your kid is out of line? Instead of ignoring or denying these signs, listen to them, and trust them. They are letting you know that it's time to take action.

FOUR: Develop a little self-confidence, honestly! You deserve to be treated with respect and kindness. If you are not sure this is true, just fake it till you make it. But of course it's true. I mean, really.

FIVE: Let your kid hear herself. This will not work for everyone, but it did for two of my most awesome friends, and you might want to try it as well. The next time your kid is treating you to an entrée of sass with sides of disrespect and obnoxiousness, flip on your phone and record the whole thing. Then tell her, "Just so you know, this is how you sound," and play it back. She may be shocked to realize how horribly she is speaking and immediately shape up—then again, she may not, in which case you'll want to finish this chapter after all.

With all this in mind, find a neutral time and settle in for a talk with your kid. You can do this at home, at a quiet café, in her room at bedtime with the lights dimmed—anywhere that feels nonthreatening and allows you to focus on each other. Tell your kid that you're unhappy with the way the two of you have been speaking to each other and that you want to work together to make things better. Don't be accusatory or launch into a tirade about how disrespectfully she's been treating you, even if she deserves it—but do let her know that the days of sassing you are over. You can say something like, "I love you, and I want you to share how you're feeling with me—but I also respect myself too much to let anyone call me stupid or roll their eyes when I'm talking, even you. Let's come up with ways you can let me know that you're angry or upset without behaving disrespectfully." Ideally your kid will warm to the subject, especially if you ask sincerely if you ever make her feel ridiculed or mocked, and the two of you can decide on phrases, gestures, and tones that are off-limits. If, however, your kid refuses to take the subject seriously, or greets your overtures with more back talk, don't engage—just tell her that you're disappointed with her response and give her a brief overview of the changes you expect.

As intimidating as it might seem, this conversation is actually the easy part! The hard part is what comes next: calmly, consistently, and firmly reinforcing this discussion with your kid. Even if you have, like, the nicest, most bonding-y talk ever, your kid will still pull out the forbidden phrases, gestures, and tones from time to time—and if the talk didn't go all that smoothly (in which case you should try again in a week or two), you might even see your kid's sassiness intensify as she tries to figure out if you really meant what you said. But your job is the same; when your kid sasses you, look her in the eye and say, "That is disrespectful, and you may not talk to me that way." Give her a chance to make it right; but if she continues in the same tone or tries to make you feel guilty for standing up for yourself ("Oh, great, Mom, thanks! So you don't even want to talk to me now?"), tell her calmly, "I can see you're upset, and I want to help you. Let me know when you're ready to speak respectfully so we can sit down together," and just disengage. You can go into another room, you can turn on some (loud) music, you can call a friend (this may seem counterintuitive, but the prospect of another adult overhearing her theatrics will actually shut your kid up fast)—whatever gives you a sense of safety and authority, as well as a break from your kid.

If uttering these phrases feels unnatural, by all means adapt them a bit—but stay brief, matter-of-fact, and to the point. If it's just the delivery you dread, try practicing in front of a mirror, or even on your partner (it's actually pretty helpful, and can lead to all kinds of naughty fun if you are twisted enough), until the words flow. And while I am not saying this will work the first, the second, or even the third time, soon enough your kid will learn that you mean business—a fact that will secretly relieve and delight her and that will improve your relationship immeasurably. Once the two of you are communicating respectfully, you will be amazed to find how much more both of you enjoy that communication and how many more things you will find to share and discuss. Possibly among your favorite new topics: rude and horrible things your kid has overheard her friends saying to their parents. The minute she starts imitating her best friend rolling her eyes and mocking her dad, you'll know your kid has turned the corner for good.

In the meantime, however, stay strong. It may help to examine your kid's outbursts from an anthropologist's point of view: What is your kid really upset about? What frustrations or insecurities is she giving voice to by sassing you? While understanding her behavior in a larger context does not excuse the behavior, it will help you take what she says less personally, as well as enable you to address her bigger issues in a more effective way. It will also keep you from getting drawn into a power struggle with your kid—saying things like, "You can't talk to me that way!" (every time she talks to you that way), or tossing some rudeness and sarcasm her way in a woefully misguided attempt to regain your authority and show her who's boss. (Hint: The boss is usually the serene, collected one, not the angry blowhard sputtering, "I don't see how I'm the idiot when I'm the only one in this room who understands sixth grade math.")

And before I let you go—just a quick word about "I hate you." I am aware that yelling "I hate you!" is supposed to be a rite of passage among tweens and that parents are supposed to absorb it with a smile and adoringly answer, "I know that you're angry with me," or "Even if you hate me, I will always love you," or something equally treacly. I have to say, I am not a big fan of "I hate you." Your kid may feel this way from time to time, but feeling it is quite different from shouting it in your face with impunity. If you like being called stupid, you'll love hearing "I hate you." If you don't, well, now you know what to do.

YOUR KID WON'T PITCH IN

◆ ◆ ◆ ◆ ◆ ◆ ◆ ◆

The sink is filled with dirty dishes, there's a pile of laundry dying to be washed, something sticky has overtaken the bathroom floor, and you've just walked in the door loaded down with a million grocery bags stuffed with your kid's Hot Pockets and MiO water enhancer. Your kid looks up at you, nods a vague hello, and goes back to lolling on the couch.

People, this is not fair. Obviously it's not fair to you, a sentiment that you repeatedly mutter under your breath while glowering at your good-for-nothing kid as you put away the groceries, deal with the dishes, start the laundry, and launch an investigation into what exactly is going on in the bathroom. But it's also not fair to your kid.

I know! You're the one freezing your fingers off rearranging packages of organic edamame to make room for five-cheese Hot Pockets—how can I possibly be worried about your kid at a time like this? From where you stand, dripping with annoyance, resentment, and whatever-that-was-in-the-bathroom, he seems to be doing just f-i-n-e.

Seems to be, sure. But let's look again. First up, he's totally clueless about the fact that he's got a parent seething every time he unlocks a new warrior on Clash of Clans—a parent likely to explode quite soon in an angry, hurtful tirade, or at least vent about him on Facebook after he's gone to bed. And it may not even be entirely his fault: While you're stewing in righteous indignation about your kid's failure to get off his butt and help you unpack groceries, you may in fact have raised him to behave precisely this way.

Think back to your kid's younger days—a family dinner, for example. When you had finally gotten a chance to sit down and were ready to enjoy your perfectly cooked, organic, and delicious meal (or, if you were living in my house, your supermarket rotisserie chicken and mashed potatoes from a box, yum), and you realized you'd forgotten the salt, what transpired? You got up to get the salt, right? And what happened three minutes later when your kid accidentally dropped his fork on the floor? You got up to fetch him a clean fork, right? (Say "thank you," honey!) And what happened twenty minutes later when it was time to bring out dessert? You got up to bring out dessert, right? Hmmm.

Your kid has probably spent much of his life having things brought to him, put in their places for him, prepared for him, and purchased for him. And even though you may have realized that he's quite old enough to Do His Part Around Here, in his mind he's still a six-year-old waiting for you to bring him the glass of juice he asked for, like, ten minutes ago. It's up to you to teach him that times have changed—and to explain why and how he should be pitching in.

While having your kid pitch in is obviously great for you—who doesn't need an extra pair of hands tackling all the shit you've got to do around the house?—it's actually great for your kid as well. He may seem happy (okay, I admit he may feel happy) lounging around while, as far as he knows, a merry band of elves tends to the needs of the home—but he's missing out on an opportunity to support the team that is his family and to learn some basic skills that will serve him well in adulthood.

This is an important change to make—but no master plan is required. Please don't call a family meeting or arrange a chore wheel or craft a lecture for your kid about pulling his weight. Just jump right in. When you come home from the market, offer your kid a friendly greeting and tell him matter-of-factly, "I could use some help bringing in the groceries. Please grab the bags from the trunk and put them on the counter." If he doesn't immediately leap to your aid (and he won't the first time, I almost promise), repeat your request and stand in front of him until he does. Once he makes it off the couch and heads for your car, don't berate him for his lackluster response, and don't link this chore to the billion other things he should be doing around here, damn it; just thank him sincerely for his help. Believe it or not, he will like having you praise him and will want you to do it again—so find other opportunities for him to pitch in, and compliment him when he does.

And believe me, there are plenty of other opportunities! Once you embark on this course of action, you will be amazed at all the ways your able-bodied tween can pitch in around the house. In addition to basic tasks like setting and clearing the table, your kid should master the proper placement of each piece of silverware, the intricacies of filling salt and pepper shakers, and how to load the dishwasher in a way that maximizes its capacity and still gives your glasses a sporting chance of surviving the rinse cycle intact. Your kid can do laundry, take care of pretty much anything lawn and garden related, sweep and vacuum and dust, take out the garbage and recycling, handle all manner of schlepping and toting, and even change sheets and replace the toilet paper rolls now and then. And that's just the beginning!

Will your kid greet this development with delighted surprise? Of course not! But don't shame or guilt him for expressing a bit of dismay; he's adjusting to a new stage in life, and you can hardly blame him for looking back fondly at the halcyon days when he lounged about like the young sultan you both believed him to be. Neither, however, should you apologize or mount an in-depth discussion of the issue; the only explanation really required is, "You're old enough to contribute around the house, and we appreciate what you do," repeated as necessary. (My husband came up with the corollary, "It's a privilege to help around the house," which does not exactly enchant our kids but which we absolutely love.)

Your kid is not the only one who needs to adjust to his new role as a pitcher-inner, however. As important as it is for your kid to assume some responsibility and do his part around the house, it's important for you to treat him as a valued partner in caring for the family home. Rather than assigning your kid tasks and running out of the room to tend to a different project, or hurriedly showing your kid how to do something and reacting with annoyance when it isn't done precisely as you'd hoped, consider using your kid's newfound helpfulness as a way to bring you closer. Have him set the table while you finish up in the kitchen; hand-wash the pot you accidentally burned while he stirs the pasta; or dump the clean laundry on the dining room table and sort it together. These jobs don't demand a lot of concentration (unless you are folding shirts, which is still a mystery to me)—and they provide a fantastic opportunity for you and your kid to spend easy time together and maybe even enjoy some bonding and conversation. Your kid is much more likely to open up while the two of you are sorting recyclables than when you're turning to him at dinner and saying something inane like, "So what's up with Kate? You seem to be talking with her just about every day at pickup"—plus you've got some help with the recycling, which is great for the earth, I know, but a complete pain in the ass. If your kid isn't a big talker, let him choose some music for you to listen to while you work—you'll get at least a glimpse into his inner life, and he may even be willing to tell you which bands he's listening to these days and why.

Over time these shared tasks will pay even greater dividends. Developing the habit of pitching in will make your kid feel like part of a team, and your whole family will enjoy a sense of common purpose and esprit de corps. Your kid may even discover some new interests unrelated to electronics and the travel lacrosse team—stirring the pasta may lead to actually preparing the pasta, for example, and eventually to some simple meals. (Just this morning my son actually uttered the phrase, "Can I make pancakes for everyone?"—which would probably never have happened had he not been introduced to the glories of the kitchen via putting away glassware.)

This sense of we're-all-in-it-together is why I really, really strongly advise against linking your kid's pitching in to an allowance. An allowance turns your kid's efforts into a transaction and implies that he deserves compensation for simply doing his part for the family. It also limits you; if you're essentially paying him for cleaning his room and taking out the garbage, your kid has annoying but convincing grounds for declining to wipe down the table after dinner, even though you may have a hundred work e-mails to return and *The Bachelor* starts in fifteen minutes. And don't pretend an allowance will teach your kid the importance of fulfilling his responsibilities and earning every penny he gets; while you might like to imagine yourself virtuously withholding your kid's allowance if he fails to do his chores, you and I both know that he'll wheedle it out of you in about four minutes.

YOUR KID IS ADDICTED TO DEVICES

◆ ◆ ◆ ◆ ◆ ◆ ◆ ◆

You must be soooo sick of all these experts telling you that your kid can't spell, can't communicate face-to-face, and can't appreciate the great outdoors and shit because he's on his device, like, all the time. However, aren't you also soooo sick of your kid being on his device, like, all the time?

I know exactly how you feel, and actually so does my kid, because I explained it to him when I had him surgically removed from his tablet several months ago. The procedure was not entirely without complications, but the prognosis is excellent, and I recommend it wholeheartedly.

It's not that I totally hated my kid's device, although I like it a hell of a lot more now that he's using it only ninety minutes a day. And I am well aware that not every kid is lucky enough to have a tablet all to himself; I do not take this good fortune for granted—well, I kind of do, but I know that I shouldn't. I also acknowledge that his device enables him to accomplish many wonderful things—including but not limited to remotely turning on the DVR because his mother inexplicably left the house without setting a timer for the *Modern Family* premiere and downloading the Minecraft camping mod so we don't actually have to go camping, hooray. And as thrilled as I am with this new dynamic, I do confess that my kid is not eagerly filling his tablet-free twenty-two and a half hours a day with family bonding activities (which is just as well, because I'm busy tweeting a photo of my sleeping dog) or organizing kickball games with the neighborhood kids (all of whom are home using their own devices).

Even still, I love having My. Kid. Off. His. Device. Wouldn't you?

I will spare you the long-winded stories about the besties I know who spent an entire hour texting one another rather than speaking—even though they were sitting like five feet apart—and the time we drove across a bridge over the bay at sunset and literally had to scream at a tween passenger to get her to look up from her phone and check out the amazing colors ("cool," she remarked and immediately returned to her device), and the fact that since tablets were permitted to students at my kid's middle school, pickup football games and rounds of Horse have given way to huddling around an iPad watching "Will It Blend?" on YouTube. If you have not been living in an ashram the past few years, and maybe even then, you must have similar tales—and a similar sense that something has gone badly awry.

What exactly is it about seeing your kid tethered to his device that bothers you so much? Is it the fact that he's physically present but mentally a million miles away? Is it the complete lack of interest in the goings-on around him implied by his constant use of his phone? Is it the gnawing concern that he may be leaving a trail of photos, comments, and messages that he'll regret when he's applying for college or a job in the not-so-far-away years? Is it just that it seems so obnoxious for a twelve-year-old to be doing whatever he wants whenever he wants on a piece of technology that costs more than the average adult in Somalia makes in a year? (I'm serious, look it up.)

If your answer is "all of the above," I am totally with you. But I do have one more question: If it bothers you so much, why is your kid still sitting there staring at his device?

Please, please rid yourself of the notion that you've got no standing to limit your kid's access to his device. Sure, he loves it. Sure, it serves many useful purposes (see *Modern Family*, on the previous page). Sure, his friends are all glued to their own devices. But remember: You're the parent. And while you may be loath to accept the privileges that come with that role—especially when exercising said privileges might make your kid, you know, disappointed or sad or angry—they are there for the taking. So take them already.

Know that this advice holds even if you remember being hugely annoyed with your parents when you were twelve and they limited your access to the phone. I am sure you fought mightily against this injustice and swore not to perpetrate such cruelty on your own offspring someday—but ha. While you might want to identify more with your cool social kid than with your hugely annoying mom, who was always haranguing you to get off the phone just when Lisa was about to disclose whether Jeff had said he liked you or not, the fact is that you are not twelve anymore. It's long past time to step into the not-so-fabulous-but-very-practical shoes of your mother and embrace your role as a setter of restrictions and a sayer of no.

Honestly, the situation is very different, anyway. Unless you were lucky (spoiled?) enough to have your own phone, you likely did not see using the phone as an inalienable right, nor (I can only assume) did you carry the phone around and give it your full attention, like, ten hours a day. Nor was the phone a gateway to an inner life completely unfamiliar to and unregulated by your parents; you may have thought whispering into the phone or taking the phone into your bedroom and locking the door kept things private, but that was nothing compared to the deleted texts, secret Snapchat and Vine accounts, and online aliases your kid might have going on his device. And while your tween self may have been occasionally blindsided by a prank call or a conversation that took a disturbing twist, at least you didn't have to worry that pushing the wrong button would take you to a website filled with pictures of giant penises (which reminds me, if you are living in the Midwest and looking for the nearest Big Boy family restaurant location, do not Google "Big Boy" and expect anything good to happen).

So yeah, you have every right and every reason to limit your kid's access to his device. And exercising that right doesn't even have to be some big traumatic deal. I'm not saying your kid will be initially thrilled with the situation—but I am saying that, handled properly, restricting your kid's screen time can lead to important conversations, meaningful sharing, and maybe even a stronger bond between you and your kid. Let's get started.

First, talk with your kid. This does not mean announcing that you're taking away his tablet because he's been on it for three hours and needs some fresh air and, come on, let's go for a walk together and you can tell me if your grade has picked up in social studies. Nor does it mean launching into a diatribe against his using devices, approaching him as if he's in trouble, or totally slamming his phone, literally or figuratively. Rather, begin positively. Encourage your kid to do most of the talking, and (silently) remind yourself to really listen to what your kid has to say. Ask him why he likes his device, what he gets out of it, what he uses it for, how it makes his life more interesting or challenging or fun. Ask him to show you his favorite apps or how he does certain things—editing photos, for example, or sharing memes. As long as you approach the subject in a friendly, open way—not a trying-to-catch-you-doing-something-bad way—he will probably be glad to have this conversation, and you may learn not just about your kid's cyberlife but even some useful tech tips.

Now it's time to deepen the conversation. Does your kid know anyone who spends too much time on a device? He probably does, and he may even be willing to tell you about it. Why does he think this person spends so much time on his tablet or phone? What might the kid be covering up? What might the kid be missing out on? Your kid is not stupid—he'll realize pretty quickly that you're not interested in his friend's online life as much as you're interested in his own—but the dynamic set up by this conversation is really helpful. It makes you a team and gives you a sense of working together to understand someone else's problem rather than opposing each other or casting blame.

It will now come as no surprise to your kid that you are going to be limiting his use of devices. Even as you're delivering the news, however, try to keep your kid engaged and the lines of communication open. You don't need to mount a huge justification for putting restrictions in place, but it's nice to provide a clear explanation and to emphasize that the limits are not intended as a punishment. And while you are obviously the final authority on how much screen time he'll be allowed and under what circumstances, let him contribute thoughts and ideas on how to make it work. While making the dining table a device-free zone is pretty basic, how do you and he feel about devices in the car? Should his time reading articles online or visiting educational sites be restricted, or just watching videos and using social media? Should you have a set number of hours per day or week he can use his device, or should he be allowed to charge it three times a week and just use it until the battery powers down? If he is in the right mood, your kid may share some pretty good insights and ideas—and even if he gets hostile or seems to shut down, he'll still recognize and appreciate that you're seeking his opinion.

Here's the kicker: Your kid may even be relieved. Because as exciting as it is to have constant access to technology, to be able to communicate with friends twenty-four/seven, to keep up, via social media and texting, with everything going on with everyone he knows—it's also pretty overwhelming. If your kid is using his device to communicate with pals—and he almost certainly is, a lot of the time—he's never able to disentangle himself from the challenges, the drama, and the crises of life with his peer group.

I can tell you the day my tween son stopped harassing me about getting a phone: It was the day we had friends visiting from out of town, and their kid spent most of our time together glued to his phone, growing more and more upset as he followed a series of texts in which classmates argued over which kids were genuinely liked by the alpha of their group and which were just annoying hangers-on. It was pretty awful, and my kid—who is not easily swayed from wanting what he wants—did not mention getting a phone for several months afterward, which in tween time is like an eternity. Don't you remember how great it felt to come home after a shitty day in middle school and shut the door behind you? Your kid, who is always connected to his classmates via texting and social media, no longer has that option—unless you give it to him.

But even if your kid's not relieved—or won't admit it—some good will still come out of these discussions. They open the door to examining issues even bigger than devices—issues like sometimes having different rules than his friends do and understanding what values are conveyed by the limits you set. I'm not saying your kid will immediately embrace these rules and values, but knowing that your decisions are not arbitrary, and knowing that they reflect deeper convictions than going-along-with-the-group or succeeding-socially or what-happens-online-stays-online, is actually very reassuring. And it will help a lot if you put some limits on your own technology as well: Your kid is probably as sick of having you respond to his questions or statements with, "What? Let me finish this text, then I can listen," as you are of him failing to put down his phone when you talk. You both could probably use a reminder that the world is wider than a screen, that there is some great non-device stuff to do out there—and maybe, if you're finished commenting on my Instagram photo of the awesome sushi I had for lunch, you could even do it together.

YOUR KID IS BANKRUPTING YOU

◆ ◆ ◆ ◆ ◆ ◆ ◆ ◆

How long has it been since you splurged on a new handbag? I mean a handbag for you, by the way, not the totally cute purse you just bought your kid because it matched the spangly gladiator sandals she fell in love with at the mall. And how long, while I'm asking, has it been since you purchased some spangly gladiator sandals for yourself?

Actually, if you are buying spangly gladiator sandals for yourself, you may need more help than this book can offer. The point, however, still stands: Chances are that you are spending a far larger percentage of your income on little—or not-so-little—treats for your kid than on yourself. And that, my friend, needs to change.

Now, I realize that kids are expensive. I have three myself; and while I adore them with my entire being, even I, their besotted parent, must admit that they have done little to enhance our family's financial bottom line. Of course your kid needs to eat and be clothed and enjoy a few privileges and niceties; and of course paying for these necessities will drain quite a bit of your funds. You will also find that saving for your kid's future is often at odds with booking passage on a cruise to Alaska or buying that lake house you've always dreamed of, but that's what you signed on for when you decided to have a kid, and you've just got to suck it up.

However. Feeding and sheltering your kid is an entirely different matter than keeping her in the latest fashions; and giving up waterfront property so she can go to college is not the same thing as scrimping and extreme couponing so you can pay for two extra weeks of horseback riding camp. And the time has arrived to explain these facts to the bottomless pit that your kid has become.

Say it with me: "That sounds great, but we can't afford it." Hey, I told you to say it with me—not run away and hide! Yes, it's hard to do the first time, but sharing the fact that you are not an endless well of cash is an important thing to do with your kid. You're still hiding, aren't you? Okay, stay under the bed for another minute or two—but at least listen while I explain further.

Your kid almost certainly suspects that your financial situation is not the stuff of her dreams. Even if you think you make a good living, have a nice house, and shower her with everything her little heart desires, the fact is that she has richer friends with bigger allowances, better rooms, and far more shit than you could ever dream of. I know this is a tough realization to accept. Our society places so much emphasis on wealth and acquisition that admitting we can't afford something makes us feel like flops. And when that "something" is a pair of pricey sneakers half your kid's class already has, a vacation to rival that of her best friend (my kid's friends have been to significantly more European capitals than I have, so believe me, I know how you feel), or an awesome tricked-out bedroom when your kid feels she's basically living in a closet (my kid again, and her room is actually kind of small), it's easy to feel even worse—as if you're letting your kid down in some terrible way.

It's kind of depressing to make this realization, I know—but it's also kind of liberating. Knowing that you will never, ever be able to buy your kid everything she wants means that you're going to disappoint her eventually—so why not do it before she pushes you even further along the road to bankruptcy? And why not tell her explicitly what she already knows—that your money is a finite thing, and that she's not the only one entitled to it—and maybe even delve deeper into the subject?

First, drop the contrite or defensive attitude. Yes, it's tough for your kid not to have a top-of-the-line phone when many of her friends do, and yes, it's hard for her not to enjoy a shopping spree every couple of weekends when her friends are sporting new outfits, like, every day—but these difficulties are part of life rather than something you need to apologize for. Nor should you feel guilty for not making these extras your top priority; forgoing a mani-pedi with a friend so that you can buy your kid yet another fuzzy sweater and a zebra-print rucksack or giving your kid the new tablet you just bought and making do with the old one (true story!) will not only give your kid a completely skewed sense of how the universe operates and an even more bloated sense of entitlement, but will also doom you to chipped nails, a slower Wi-Fi connection—and, oh yeah, resentment of your kid. This is where "That sounds great, but we can't afford it" comes in—delivered not in a glum, remorseful way but in a casual, matter-of-fact, end-of-story tone.

Make sure, however, that you don't go so far in the antiapology direction that you drift into defensiveness or antagonism. Unless your kid is trying to make you feel guilty or inadequate when you suggest she find a way to cope with her hair that does not involve regular salon appointments and weekly blowouts, there's no need to answer her request with a list of the million things you've bought her in the past month and an angry reminder that you work hard and deserve to enjoy a few luxuries yourself, has she stopped to think about that? Once again, "That sounds great, but we can't afford it" will serve you well. Because it probably does sound great, and you probably can empathize with the feeling of wanting something beyond your means—and there's no shame in acknowledging both of these facts to your kid.

As fantastic a phrase as "That sounds great, but we can't afford it" may be, however, don't let it stand as the only thing you say to your kid when it comes to money. Your kid is old enough to learn about costs, budgeting, and saving—and the values your family upholds when making financial decisions. If you use online coupons or clip them from the Sunday paper, for example, involve your kid in the routine; let her search the Internet for bargains (not only will she enjoy the task, but she'll also find websites and deals you never knew existed) or set her up with some scissors and go through the coupon inserts together. Rather than doing the grocery shopping while she's at school (even though she's told you a million times she hates the market, I know), drag her along and have her practice her math skills by figuring out the price per serving and price per unit of various items. Tell her why you shop the way you do; if you save by buying generic peanut butter, for example, but shell out for non-GMO dairy or locally grown produce or name-brand cereal, share the reasoning behind your choices—and let her weigh in, too. Do the same when considering family outings or major purchases; without disclosing your net worth or giving her TMI about your finances, you can still help her understand just how many dinners out you might have to forgo in order to upgrade her phone or how many extra hours the average American worker would need to put in to cover the cost of her ballet costume for the spring recital. Once she's gotten the hang of budgeting—and understands the link between what you spend and what you value—put her in charge of planning a day trip for under twenty dollars per person (don't forget to include the cost of gas!) or selecting ingredients for three nights' worth of dinners or deciding what luxuries she wants to give up in return for getting a new set of earbuds just like the ones everyone else has, really, everyone.

I'm not saying that these activities will end your kid's I-want-that-itis, or that she'll immediately jump on the clip-and-save train, but I am saying that they will help your kid understand that you are more than a large, occasionally cranky ATM and that your saying no to her requests for treats and luxuries is not just you being mean or cheap or poor. I'm also saying that you should not feel embarrassed about providing her with less than her wealthier, or just being-raised-with-different-values, friends may enjoy, and that the tween years are exactly the right time for introducing her to issues like budgeting and finances rather than shielding her from such matters completely.

And finally, I am saying that you definitely deserve a new handbag more than your kid needs a purse to match her new shoes. But if I see you even trying on those hideous gladiator sandals, I am seriously never speaking to you again.

YOUR KID NEVER DOES ANYTHING NICE FOR YOU

◆ ◆ ◆ ◆ ◆ ◆ ◆ ◆

You spend most of your waking hours doing stuff for your kid, and that's not even counting all the sleep you lost not-so-many years ago wiping his poopy bottom in the middle of the night. Of course taking care of him is an honor and privilege, but it's also a real time suck and often not all that fun. Especially when your birthday rolls around and what you get from your kid is a muttered "Happy birthday" and his sullen, texting presence at your celebratory dinner.

You're so nice to your kid—how can you get him to do something nice for you?

There's nothing like a sulky tween rolling his eyes when you're blowing out the candles on the birthday cake you ordered and picked up from the bakery yourself to make you nostalgic for the long-ago days when your kid couldn't do enough for you. Remember those painstakingly lettered "I love you, Mommy! Happy birthday!" missives, his doomed but loving attempts to present you with breakfast in bed, and the rolls of Scotch tape that gave their lives so he could wrap your present all by himself? How did that sweet little guy morph into this uncaring grouch claiming to be your offspring?

Yes, your kid's being sort of a jerk—but take a deep breath before throwing his phone in the toilet and launching into a lecture about how much better he should be treating his mom, or locking yourself in the bathroom before he can see your eyes brimming with tears at his shoddy treatment of you, his once-beloved parent. I know it's your birthday, and I'm not trying to be mean, but is it possible that maybe he's not the only one to blame for this obnoxious behavior? Is it possible that in your quest to be the all-loving, all-giving parent you thought you were supposed to be, you actually taught your kid to treat your big day—and you—exactly this way?

Think back, way back, to those special occasions when your kid went out of his way to do something nice for you. You thanked him profusely, right? You felt loved and happy and appreciative, right? But I'll bet you also felt a little bit guilty—guilty that your kid had burned himself on the toaster, made you a present of a piece of candy or a pretty rock that you knew he wanted for himself, or gotten frustrated and tangled up in tape. We're so conditioned to see parenting as a self-sacrificing experience that we actually feel guilty when our kids do any sacrificing themselves. So along with the smiles and hugs and kisses we bestow on our small children when they do nice things for us, we bestow sentiments like, "Oh, sweetie! You didn't have to do that!" or "I love my card, but I hope you didn't use up all your drawing paper making it for me!" or "That candy looks so delicious that I want you to have it!" And we can't blame our kids for hearing these words—and internalizing the message they convey.

The message is this: Don't go to any trouble for me. And unlike your spouse, to whom you say this but who damn well better know you don't mean it, your kid takes the message at face value. So as he gets older, and the urge to make colorful birthday cards and experiment with the toaster wanes, he just goes with it. By the time he's progressed from toddler to kid to tween, he's grown accustomed to doing exactly what you asked: not doing anything nice for you.

And not to pile it on, but your kid probably has no idea how much those early forays into doing-nice-things-for-Mom meant to you. Sure, you thanked him profusely—but didn't you also thank him profusely for doing shit that you actually appreciated not at all? Your kid spent his formative years hearing you chirp, "Thank you, honey!" as he handed you snot-soaked tissues and crushed juice boxes to throw away, for heaven's sake. How is he supposed to know that watching him sulk through your birthday meal is not the greatest joy of your life? How is he supposed to know that you want more?

Well, it's time to let your kid know.

To change the dynamic between you and your kid, you've got to begin by changing yourself. (Totally unfair, I realize, that getting your kid to be nicer to you means more work for you—but unlike collecting those disgusting tissues and leaking juice boxes, this work will prove gratifying.) Specifically: You've got to get rid of the pervasive notion that good parents give, give, give and ask for nothing in return. You've got to banish the nagging sense of guilt that comes with expecting your kid to go out of his way for you. And you've got to believe that you deserve a modicum of the same kindness, benevolence, and goodwill with which you've spent the past decade showering your kid.

While birthdays and other special occasions may bring into sharp focus the fact that it's time for some improvements around here, the transformation can be accomplished only through everyday behaviors. This is good news because there's no need to wait until your birthday rolls around again—you can start making the change as soon as you want, even before you've finished scarfing your leftover cake and despairing of ever fitting into the size two dress your mean-girl sister-in-law sent as a present. There's also no need for a big heart-to-heart talk with your kid or a family meeting to discuss the situation. You just basically start. Here's how:

Situation: You and your kid are about to enter a store.

Old You: Open the door and hold it for your kid.

New You: Step aside so your kid gets to the door first. As he looks up quizzically to figure out why the door is closed even though he clearly wants to go inside, smile and say, "Would you mind getting the door for us?" Go inside first, then tell him, "That was really polite. Thank you."

Situation: You and your kid are leaving the store, but it's started to rain outside.

Old You: Run and get the car, then pull up to the curb so your kid won't get wet.

New You: If your kid were old enough to drive, I'd tell you to have him bring the car around. Until that day, however, tell your kid, "Wow, it's wet! Looks like we'd better run for it." (Yes, you'll both end up sopping, but you'll also send the message that you and your kid are in this together.) When you get home, ask your kid to bring you a towel and/or to microwave two glasses of milk so you can make hot chocolate after you lock up the car.

Situation: You are grabbing a rare moment of peace on the couch while your kid loiters around the kitchen looking for Doritos. You want a Diet Coke.

Old You: Get up and get a Diet Coke, of course, or sit there wishing you weren't feeling too comfortable to get up and get a Diet Coke.

New You: Call out, "Sweetie, could you please bring me a Diet Coke? Thank you so much!"

These may seem like small matters—although having someone bring you a Diet Coke while you loll on the sofa is truly one of life's great pleasures—but each of these exchanges actually helps foster a new relationship between you and your kid. In a friendly, casual, nonthreatening way, they chip away at the assumption that you give to your kid rather than the other way around. They enable you to ask your kid to do something nice for you without making yourself vulnerable. And they get your kid in the habit of thinking about your wants and needs and how he can look out for you.

I know what you're thinking: These interactions are too artificial, right? They're totally staged. You don't want your kid to do nice stuff for you just because you've asked or because you've somehow trained him to do so. You only want your kid to do what comes from the heart.

This, no offense, is complete bullshit. If you stand around waiting for your kid's heart to move him to open that door for you, you're going to be stuck there all fucking day. Sure, eventually these nice things your kid is doing will come from the heart—but that just doesn't happen right away. And in the meantime, nice stuff is nice stuff whether it comes from the heart or not. Think about it: If you hadn't wiped his long-ago poopy bottom until your heart moved you to do so, your kid could still be lying on that changing pad.

And really, why not assume that your kid won't actually hate doing nice stuff for his mom, and that he'll approach this new dynamic with a willing spirit? If you give your kid the opportunity and the tools to be nice to you, he could surprise you with his enthusiasm. After all, the little kid who crafted all those cards and wrapped all those rocks is still in there somewhere; he might enjoy making an encore appearance after so many years.

Just a quick note if your kid is already in the habit of opening doors, bringing things, and helping out—just not for you: People, please. Do not fall prey to the illusion that your kid's being a considerate citizen in public liberates him from displaying the same consideration at home. If your kid is routinely earning props from his teachers, his coaches, and the parents of his friends for going above and beyond, this means that he is more than ready to start doing some nice stuff for you as well. Of course you should allow your kid to "relax" and "be himself" at home—but this is not the same as encouraging him to unveil his most self-centered and negligent qualities while you wait with increasing desperation for him to treat you as thoughtfully as he allegedly treats Dillon's mom.

And when your birthday comes around again? Hopefully by then, your kid will know what to do—but if you're not sure, enlist a spouse or a friend to remind your kid about your special day and offer to help him plan a fun surprise. Breakfast in bed and a dress that you can actually fit into might be a nice start.

YOUR KID DOESN'T CARE ABOUT HIS RELATIVES

◆ ◆ ◆ ◆ ◆ ◆ ◆ ◆

It's time for a family reunion! Your Facebook feed is crammed with snaps of your friends' beaming kids hugging cousins and wrapping their arms around wizened relatives ("Feeling blessed!" cheer the status reports. "Happy times!")—so you know this is going to be totally idyllic. You charge the phone to record your own joyful moments and share them with everyone you know, prepare and pack and schlep, finally tumble out to see the extended family, and wait for the magic to unfold.

And wait. Because, to be perfectly honest, you're not feeling all that blessed.

Maybe you've forgotten that a family gathering will require you to actually spend time with the snarky tween who's taken over your adorable child's body. Maybe that shot of him slouching on the couch and installing new apps as great-aunt Ida shares stories of her recent bowel procedure is not the one you envisioned accompanying your own "Happy times!" post. And maybe, as you look around the motley crew that are your closest relations and try to see things from your kid's point of view, you're suddenly willing to give him a pass on engaging with these people.

Your kid's clearly uncomfortable. Too old to snuggle up to Grandma and delightedly munch on vanilla caramels, too young to feign fascination with Uncle Scott's strange opinions on climate change and the integrity of the nation's food supply, too cool to join in the smaller cousins' games of Uno and Battleship, your kid is hardly Instagram ready. In fact, he seems so thoroughly miserable that you're feeling guilty for dragging him here in the first place. After all, you're not crazy about great-uncle Harold, either, and it seems so mean to force your kid to make conversation with relatives he has, like, nothing in common with and who spit when they talk. You know logically that your kid is lucky to have extended family to visit and that the ancestral bond is primal and essential and stronger than water or whatever and that, when he's older, he'll appreciate the memories (if not the photos) of these gatherings—but in the meantime, why not just leave him alone?

Here's why: Flash forward a few decades, and that doddering, irritating relative will be you—and the kid avoiding the seat beside you and ignoring your clumsy attempts to connect will be your beloved grandchild or great-nephew. And Future You will think back to the day you let your kid ignore his extended family because, well, you can't remember exactly why, but it seemed like a good enough reason at the time—and you will desperately wish you had made a different choice. Because the attitude you display today is the attitude you will instill in your kid—and the attitude that he will instill in his own kids, your unborn but sure-to-be-awesome-and-precious grandchildren—about the importance of intergenerational familial relationships.

Yes, extended family reunions can be awkward; yes, your kid may be ill at ease; yes, your relatives may be odd and annoying. But none of that excuses your kid from putting on a happy face and trying his best to be a smiling, sunny presence. I understand that this is not the news your kid wants to hear—but it's the right thing to do, and on some level both of you know it.

It's also not the worst thing in the world to make nice with people who love you, so try to remain a smiling, sunny presence yourself. Don't denigrate your relatives or act like your kid is doing the world's biggest favor by actively participating in a visit with his extended family; just remind him to be polite and to give his full attention to the people around him. If you can guide the conversation toward tidbits that will spark your kid's interest, that is great—many older people have captivating stories to tell, and your kid may surprise you by genuinely wanting to learn the details of your uncle's days in the military or your mother's childhood squabbles with her siblings—but remember that keeping your kid engaged and entertained is not the focal point of the proceedings.

We spend so much time trying to make life easy and pleasant for our kids that we sometimes forget there are more important values at stake. And while your kid might enjoy the family reunion a lot more if he's allowed to don his earbuds and lose himself in Vine until all the relatives have given up on engaging him in conversation and/or fallen asleep in front of the TV, he'll also miss an amazing and important opportunity to step up and develop some growth and maturity. No matter how much you try to smooth your kid's path, he's eventually going to experience situations that make him feel out of place and unsettled, scenarios that require him to flail around outside his comfort zone and find his own way. Having this experience as a tween at a family reunion—rather than as a teenager navigating his first day at a new high school, for example—is actually a pretty great opportunity. It's also a chance for your kid to realize that being part of a family means doing for others rather than just letting them do for him, and to put the feelings of other people ahead of his own.

Of course your kid has zero interest in great-aunt Ida's bowel procedure (at least, I hope so—otherwise, that's a little weird)—but tuning in and nodding sympathetically at the appropriate times will teach him not only about the wonders of the digestive system but also about handling himself in uncomfortable social situations and demonstrating respect for his elders. Of course he's way beyond cuddling with Grandma—but going out of his way to sit next to her on the couch and asking about her latest knitting project (or attempt to scale Everest, or whatever) will give him a chance to act like an adult, to practice his conversational skills, and to repay her for all those times she watched him build block towers and listened to him blather endlessly about dinosaurs. And of course a game of Battleship with his sticky young cousins is about as appealing a prospect as actually going down with the destroyer, but joining in a few rounds will hone his leadership, patience, and appreciation for the trials of managing and entertaining children.

Hopefully these encounters will lead to some sweet, meaningful moments between your kid and his relatives (keep your phone charged and ready for pics!)—often, extended family members are the ones best able to see the adorable child hiding inside your snarky tween's body and to coax him out to play. You can also build on these connections by sharing family lore, old photos, and the like with your kid, and by encouraging him to reach out to his grandparents, aunts, uncles, and cousins even if the next family reunion may be years away. But no matter how blissfully happy, completely unmoved, or totally irked your kid appears by the time spent with his relatives, know that you are planting important seeds for your kid's long-term development—as a family member, as an adult, and yes, as a future parent and a link between the generations.

And speaking of family gatherings, your kid's role as a smiling, sunny presence need not be limited to a triannual multigenerational reunion. No doubt your Facebook feed also sports images of parents and children seemingly delighting in one another's company for a regular "Pancake breakfast!" or "Nature walk!" or "Movie and sushi night!" While the actual content of these special outings may not in fact live up to the photos (I can personally attest that one of my favorite happy-family-on-the-beach shots was captured the only minute someone was not crying or sulking, including me), the pictures do serve as a reminder that even as the parent of a tween, you are still entitled to experience some family fun every now and then. I realize that your kid might disagree, and that his disagreement might be accompanied by enough eye rolls, heavy sighs, and sarcastic remarks to tempt you to forget the whole thing—but don't give up! If your kid can be expected to buck up and put on a happy face for a family reunion, he can damn well put on a happy face and act like he's enjoying the occasional outing with you and whoever else you're dragging along. He can't possibly be as miserable having a picnic with the family or going to the planetarium as you were spending all those Saturday mornings providing organic granola bars and seedless oranges for his peewee soccer league, and you always maintained a beatific smile, right? So now it's his turn.

You may wish to express this fact to your kid in a slightly more positive way: "I understand that you'd rather stay home, or play Skyrim, or die, or whatever, than go on a family hike, but that's the plan for today. I'm looking forward to it, and I think we can have a great time. Your job is to show a good attitude and really try to have fun," followed if necessary by, "Not everything our family does is going to be your favorite, just like not everything we do is my favorite. But I support the things that are important to you, and I expect you to do the same without complaining and sulking." You definitely have the moral high ground here, so stay strong. And post a pic on Facebook to let me know how it goes.

YOUR KID DOESN'T CARE ABOUT OTHERS

◆ ◆ ◆ ◆ ◆ ◆ ◆ ◆

Oh my gosh, your kid is so endlessly fascinating. I love hearing all about her dance team and her skirmishes with the jealous girls at school and the fact that she totally deserved an A on her history fair project; thanks again for tweeting the photo so I could see for myself. It must be amazing to be the parent of such an outstanding and incredible tween—actually, I know for sure that it is, because you tell me, like, all the time. So I feel terrible for bringing this up, but I can't help asking: Um, isn't your kid awfully preoccupied with herself?

I know your kid's life is extremely exciting, but I'm starting to wonder if she ought to have a few interests besides what's going on in it. Because while classes and sports and extracurriculars and friends and what she wants for dinner and how much her siblings (not to mention you) are annoying her and her countdown to being old enough to wear mascara at school are definitely enough to fill your kid's days, these days might be a lot more meaningful if she got out of her own head every now and then.

Here's a heartwarming anecdote: A friend of mine is pretty socially engaged, the type who reads online articles about breaking the cycle of poverty and providing access to affordable health care while I'm busy following people on Pinterest and participating in Throwback Thursday. Anyway, she grew concerned about the plight of hungry kids in the community and decided to launch a food drive in her kid's school. When she met with the school's parent council—which totally coincidentally doubles as the school's clique of alpha moms—to try to get the ball rolling, she was greeted with skepticism and disdain. "I don't know what you're talking about," one mom sniffed, gesturing at the pristine school grounds and groups of students strolling from art class to water polo practice and stuff like that. "I don't see any hunger in our community."

If you don't want your kid to be that mom in twenty-five years (although it would be fabulous if she could have that mom's skin and pedi, I mean, wow), it's time to broaden your kid's horizons a bit. And don't feel bad that she'll require some help with this project; though over the years you've sent scads of well-deserved opportunities to excel and shine your kid's way, she may not have been given all that many chances to expand her sphere of concern. Empathy is a learned skill, after all, one difficult to acquire in an environment that centers largely on catering to your kid's every whim and celebrating her every action. But even though she may be strolling down the path of, shall we say, self-preoccupation, it is definitely not too late for your kid.

While nagging and complaining about your kid are always

popular tools for attempting to change her behavior, they won't be all that useful here. (Or anywhere, but that's what the other chapters in this book are for.) The best way to get your kid on board with thinking about others is simply to set a good example. This may be hard to believe, as these days your kid appears drawn by demonic forces to do the exact opposite of whatever you are doing, and I'm not saying the tactic will work when it comes to not rolling her eyes when people talk or not insisting on wearing body glitter to Grandpa's birthday dinner; but in this particular case, it's definitely the way to go.

If you're anything like my socially aware friend, setting a good example is a cinch: Talk about the issues that are troubling you, explain what you are doing about them and why, and invite your kid's opinion and involvement. While your kid may not be ready to understand all the details and nuances of the problems with which you're engaged, she does have a well-developed concept of right versus wrong and fair versus unfair, and she may surprise you by displaying an immediate and passionate interest in topics like child hunger, education for girls in other countries, clean water, the environment, and endangered species. She probably also has a flair for drama and action, which can easily be channeled into efforts to further whatever causes are most important to you and your family.

But what if you're more the Pinterest-and-Throwback-Thursday type? Then maybe it's time to consider the example you're setting for your kid. It's kind of hard to fault your kid for being selfish if she never sees you write a check to a charity, participate in civic activism beyond complaining about Congress, or extend yourself on behalf of your community's less advantaged members. You can't just tell your kid to think of others—you've got to show her that you do. And if you don't, well, this is a good time to start.

Just keeping your life and family organized is consuming enough, I totally understand. I went to a mother-daughter book club at my kid's school recently; to open the discussion, the facilitator asked the moms and girls to tell one another about our favorite activities. From the girls immediately poured forth a stream of answers—gymnastics, dance, reading, shopping, helping out around the house (kidding! Would have been awesome, though). Many of the moms, however, were totally stymied. Favorite activities? Since driving carpool and getting the occasional facial did not seem to be what the facilitator was looking for, most of us were out of luck.

So, no, I'm not telling you to turn your backyard into a homeless shelter or foster a hundred abandoned cats (I mean, yuck) or jet off to build a school in Tanzania. But I am suggesting that the next time you're stopped at a traffic light with a carload of silently texting tweens, or relaxing under a mask of seaweed, yogurt, and avocado, you remember the change-the-world-and-save-the-planet college student you used to be and ask her for some advice. Just because your impulses for community service and making a difference have been buried under years of being-an-adult-and-becoming-a-parent doesn't mean they're not still in there, and it will be great not only for your kid but also for you if you dig them up. Revisit the causes that used to inspire you, or consider new ones that might move you; once you hit on the right issue, you'll be surprised how easy it is to find some time and energy to devote to it.

And in the meantime, you can do lots of little things that add up to a bigger value. When it's time for back-to-school shopping, for example, stop fighting with your kid about shoes long enough to pick up some new binders, notebooks, and clothes to donate to local students in need. Ditto for holiday shopping; work with your kid to compose not just her own wish list but also a list of items your family could provide for a less fortunate kid her age. Place a box in the pantry for collecting canned goods, and add to it every time there's a good buy-one-get-one sale at the grocery store; or invite your kid to join you in writing letters of support or making greeting cards for hospitalized patients and soldiers serving overseas. And don't forget to comb carefully through outgrown clothes or less used toys and appliances; rather than just sticking them in the garage or schlepping them all to Goodwill, pick out the nicest items and do a little research to determine where they'll do the most good and bring the most joy.

Along the way, you—or your kid—might find a passion for a particular cause. If you are superlucky, your kid will follow the path of a tween I know whose participation in a food drive led to his organizing a sale of Rainbow Loom bracelets (remember those?) to raise money for children's meals, or another kid who regularly visits a nursing home to play piano for the residents. But even if she doesn't turn into Mother Teresa, your kid will still benefit from seeing your unselfishness—and will absorb the example more than you might realize. Over time, thinking about others will become a reflex for you and your kid—and when you feel she needs a reminder (i.e., when she's trying to convince you that she's the least privileged kid in the universe because you won't spring for yet another leotard), your already-established concern for the less fortunate will give you the standing to deliver it without looking like an insincere, preachy jerk.

Not only will your kid's learning to care about others make her a better person and all that, but it will also have an immediate and practical benefit on her day-to-day life. It will help her realize that she can make a difference, that her actions matter, that she is a person of power. A lot of your kid's annoying and exasperating behaviors are centered on her desire to make an impact, her yearning for clout and control, so finding a new, positive way to influence people and events outside her immediate circle will be extremely gratifying. Having interests besides herself is also a great cushion against the social conflicts and draining emotional highs and lows that inevitably come with being an awesome tween girl; if those jealous girls turn against her, for example, life at school could get pretty dicey, and your kid will be awfully glad to know that there is a world outside dance team. A world not as sparkly, maybe, but a world nonetheless.

YOUR KID WON'T PICK UP AFTER HERSELF

◆ ◆ ◆ ◆ ◆ ◆ ◆ ◆

If you enjoy picking up your house so much that you welcome any additions to the clutter, or if you genuinely believe the three pairs of flip-flops your kid has left lying around foster a casual, happy, be-yourself atmosphere in the home, this chapter is not for you.

You're still reading, hooray. We are clearly kindred spirits, so I will share a secret with you: I really hate picking up after myself. I have fantasies about being Princess Kate, surrounded by ladies-in-waiting who keep track of my stuff, hand it to me when I want it, and then—swish!—whisk it away and stick it who-cares-where until I need it again. Seriously, that is the life. (Though not my life.) Can you imagine how awesome it must be never to put your own shit away?

While the princess may be unavailable for comment, you might still get a glimpse into such a pampered existence by observing your kid. There she is, surrounded by yet another pair of flip-flops (do they breed?), a bag of veggie chips, and various schoolbooks, electronics, papers, and writing utensils—all doomed to abrupt and total abandonment as soon as she finishes her homework. At that point, she'll move on to another activity—and you'll take your cue to swoop in and deal with the stuff she's left behind, whisking it away and sticking it who-cares-where until she needs it again. Because, you sigh, your kid never puts her own shit away.

Well. Unless your kid plans to marry into the royal family—which may cause as many problems as it solves—this situation is untenable in the long run. Her college roommate, her future domestic partner, anyone with whom your kid will share living space in the coming years is unlikely to take on the task of picking up after her with the same vim and vigor that you do. And as you're clearly ready for a rest yourself, let's get your kid acclimated to what's ahead—and teach her to put her own things away.

Instilling this habit in your kid will not only spare you physically (no matter how much you may love the dolphin and garland poses at yoga, getting on the floor to pull your kid's tie-dyed sock out from under the couch is another matter entirely) and free up some time to plan imaginary trips to exotic destinations overseas (wait, that's me), but it will also make you feel about a thousand percent better about life with your kid. While a little bit of picking up after your kid is fine—everybody leaves something behind now and then, and it's easy enough to toss *Allegiant* onto your kid's bed once in a while—regularly putting your kid's stuff away makes you feel kind of awful, doesn't it?

The task is so Sisyphean, first of all—the second you get the common areas tidied up, the second your kid launches herself at the breakfast bar, shedding empty cartons of almond milk and stray

Craisins and chewed-up straws (ick) for you to deal with while she prances off to the bathroom to straighten her hair. There's also no fun in it. I mean, loading the dishwasher is not exactly an ecstatic experience, but there is a certain satisfaction in fitting every pot in; and I am not an enthusiastic laundress, but the feel of fresh-from-the-dryer sheets is pretty awesome—but putting your kid's same shit in the same places day after day is just ungratifying and stupid. And finally, picking up after your kid breeds resentment—which is not the best thing for the already-fitful relationship between parent and tween.

It's like this: When your kid leaves her stuff lying around, she's pretty much saying that the stuff's not important enough for her to bother with and that she expects somebody else to take care of it for her. That's annoying, because she's showing a lack of regard for her things as well as for the appearance (such as it is) of your house in general. So you nag your kid to pick up after herself—which doesn't work—or you decide to let her stuff sit there until she deals with it—which also doesn't work, because your kid's indifference will inevitably win out over your desire for a coffee table unadorned by a million frayed threads from last night's foray into making friendship bracelets. So day after day, you find yourself putting your kid's stuff away—after all, there's really no other way.

Ah, but of course there is. Just ask my grandmother.

My grandmother is pretty amazing (I'm sure yours is, too, but has she ever taken teenaged you to see the Pet Shop Boys at Wembley Stadium in London, then taught you to play poker over a glass or two of wine?—just saying)—including in her strategy for keeping a tidy home. This was it: You put your stuff away, and fast, or it disappeared. Matter-of-fact and unapologetic, she'd sweep into the trash can whatever her family didn't value sufficiently to keep in its place. School projects, photos, books, socks—after a few hours or days, depending on her mood, swish, away it all went. The legend goes that my grandpa, her husband, did not realize this policy applied to him as well as to the kids until he went looking for his favorite sport coat—and learned that it had been left hanging on the dining room chair one day too many and was probably in some landfill by now. Seriously, this was one clean house.

Of course, those who actually lived with my grandmother were probably less amused to experience her technique than I was to hear about it—and I am not suggesting you adopt this exact practice in your home. However, there is a happy medium between consigning your kid's cherished crafts to the garbage can and meticulously putting away her every possession day after day—and it's called The Box.

It's really simple, and it's really, really effective. You have a box (hence the name of this operation), and every now and then you go through the house and fill it with whatever's lying around. Sneakers, half-eaten snacks, forgotten friendship bracelets, anything not in its proper place is fair game to get dumped into The Box. Then you stick The Box in an out-of-the-way spot, bask in the joy of an uncluttered home—and wait.

It won't be long before your kid notices that her (totally cute) slouchy beanie is not on its hook in her closet, nor is it lying on the ottoman where she left it yesterday, nor is it hanging from the towel rack in your bathroom, where it inexplicably lived for three days last week, and she will want it back. But since it's now in The Box, getting it back isn't so easy. You can use your imagination in developing the conditions under which your kid can reclaim something from The Box: Maybe she has to wait a week, maybe she has to put away everything else in The Box first, or maybe she has to do some extra chores—whatever works for your family. Make the procedure unpleasant enough that your kid will want to avoid it in the future—but not so punishing that she feels you don't respect her right to her things. Especially the beanie, which is really that adorable.

Unless you are a complete jerk, you'll want to give your kid plenty of advance warning before implementing The Box. The point is not to pull the rug out from under your kid by having her possessions suddenly disappear or to vent your own frustration with your kid by carelessly tossing aside stuff you know is important to her; the point is to teach her to treat her things, and her surroundings, with respect by picking up after herself. Therefore, The Box should be presented not as a punishment but as a tool to help change the situation and improve the dynamic in your home. If your kid doesn't react with hostility or defensiveness, you can even involve her in deciding how items should be redeemed from The Box, how often sweeps through the house should be made, and what she herself can do to remember to put her stuff away. In fact, a detailed discussion about The Box may motivate your kid to start picking up after herself so well that you won't even need it. In which case you'll find your home newly cluttered with a large, useless Box, a development that is sort of ironic but ultimately for the best.

YOUR KID IS BORED

◆ ◆ ◆ ◆ ◆ ◆ ◆ ◆

It's a big, beautiful world—but it's not exciting enough to interest your kid. He's bored.

You have heard him utter this phrase many times before, and you know that pursuing the topic never ends well. He will elaborate that he has nothing to do, he means it, nothing; and you will end up either fuming at your kid's insolence or mired in frustration and failure as all the fun activities you suggest to combat his boredom are proclaimed not only boring but stupid as well.

This brings up a question: Why are you trying so hard?

At some point between your own childhood and that of your kid, the simple phrase "I'm bored" ceased to be a statement and became a rallying cry. Not a rallying cry for your kid, which might actually make sense—surely a youngster of reasonably sound mind could be expected to rouse himself from his stupor and make some sort of contribution to the world around him—but a rallying cry for you. Hearing that a kid is bored triggers a reflex in most parents, a reflex rendered no less powerful by the fact that it's utterly ridiculous, a reflex to step in and do whatever it takes to stop the boredom.

Sometimes this reflex takes the form of scolding or shaming your kid. "I'd love a chance to be bored," you snap, proceeding to list the five hundred thousand things you've got to plow through before you can relax over a glass of wine, or at least manage a hot shower before snuggling in bed with your laptop and an in-box full of work e-mails as the clock strikes midnight. While venting and being cranky in general are actually among my favorite hobbies, I must regretfully concede that these behaviors do not help resolve this particular situation at all. Succeeding in getting a rise out of grouchy old mom may amuse your kid for a moment, but he's as unlikely to be moved by your tale of woe as you are by hearing me recite my own comprehensive catalog of Shit I Should Get To But Won't. And, by the way, this reaction also teaches your kid that it's your role to validate his emotions and that he doesn't have an intrinsic right to express unpleasant or darker feelings. Not that you want to raise a mopey, complaining dolt, but still, you don't need to be mean about it.

Another version of this response involves rattling off a bunch of chores your kid should be doing, and informing him that organizing the garage would certainly keep his boredom at bay. While I am all for tween labor, especially when it entails your kid's finally going through the boxes he's filled with crap from the floor of his closet, labeled "Soccer Trophies" and "Stuff to Keep," and dumped in a corner of the garage, this is really just a different way of smacking your kid down for saying he's bored. And no matter how cleverly you try to conceal the passive-aggressive nature of this reaction, you and your kid both know perfectly well that you're much more interested in punishing him for expressing his boredom than you are in enjoying a clean(er) garage.

Which brings us to option B: freak out. Why this happens is a mystery to me, but happen it does. Like, all the time. The fact that your kid is bored sends a wave of panic through you, a panic that your kid's ennui reflects badly on your worthiness as a parent, a panic that your dull personality and the tedious home environment you're apparently providing have rendered your kid's life completely dreary and monotonous. The only way to relieve your panic is to alleviate your kid's boredom—a task you dive into with zeal bordering on lunacy. "But it's a beautiful day!" you protest. "Why don't you go play outside?" Yeah, like that's what your kid plans to do. "Do you have a good book to read?" Uh, sure. Right. "Hmmm. Maybe you could play with [insert name of toy your kid has not picked up since third grade but that still lurks at the bottom of his dresser drawer] or make something out of [insert name of blocks or other building supplies that have lain scattered and abandoned under your kid's bed since he acquired his Xbox a billion years ago]." No, and no. With each failed suggestion, your level of anxiety rises; and the next thing you know, you've offered not only to get off the couch and fix your kid a snack but are practically begging him to call Liam and invite him to see a movie (you'll drive!)—all just to get your kid to stop complaining that he's bored.

Well, this is not any kind of a fantastic solution, either. Not only are you now stuck chauffeuring annoying Liam to *Step Up 44*, but your kid has learned three bad lessons: one, that he can get you to do all sorts of insane things simply by invoking the specter of boredom; two, that boredom is an emotion to be feared and quelled at all costs; and three, that he is totally incapable of coping with occasional boredom and discomfort on his own. Also that seeing a *Step Up* film is a satisfactory way to spend the afternoon, but we can deal with that one another time.

I realize I appear to have discredited every possible rejoinder to the "I'm bored!" emanating from your kid—but actually, there's one more: Don't take it so damn hard. Assume that your kid is not pronouncing judgment on your excitement factor as a parent nor recapping the whole of his life up to this point nor requesting a survey of every remotely entertaining activity within a ten-mile radius—assume that he's just expressing a thought, and react appropriately. "Yeah?" and "It sounds like you're looking for something to do," and "I'm actually kind of bored myself," are all neutral responses signaling to your kid that you care about his feelings but aren't going to get too wrapped up in them. You can even use "I'm bored" as an opening to try to connect with your kid: "I was about to take the dog for a walk. Want to come?" (If your kid is bored enough, or if complaining of boredom is his awkward attempt to open a conversation with you, you might be surprised at how well this will go.)

But what if he says no to the walk or just repeats that he's bored? Well, then, try backing off for a while. Although it's important for your kid to know that you're listening when he speaks and that you care about his inner life, it's also good for him to be able to express an emotion and have you respond with calm acceptance and equanimity rather than jump up to do something about it. We spend so much time and energy hovering over our kids, cataloging and reacting to their every flicker of mood, that we sometimes impede them from processing their own feelings and getting to know themselves. It's kind of exhausting for us, as well as deeply unfair to our kids. Honestly, your kid's boredom is sort of a gift; he rarely has the opportunity just to be still and tune in to his own feelings—and while boredom may not be his favorite feeling, it's a feeling nonetheless.

And there's nothing wrong with a little boredom, anyway: Despite our society's insistence that we go, go, go twenty-four/seven, and our discomfort with seeing people just sitting around, a bit of downtime could actually do your kid a world of good. What he sees as boredom you can recognize as a chance to unwind, a chance to chill out, a chance to enjoy the sensation of the couch against his back and the air-conditioning on his face, a chance to appreciate the awesome ceiling light fixture that took you, like, four months to find, maybe even a chance to indulge in some daydreaming or self-contemplation.

Once your kid realizes that his statement of boredom is not provoking much reaction, he'll either launch into whining, complaining mode—in which case you can serenely reply, "Yes, I heard you're bored. Let me know if you want to walk the dog together," and sidle away, or take charge of his own situation, whether by engaging you in conversation (rare, but it does happen) or lying on the aforementioned couch or eventually managing to come up with something to do.

Letting your kid accept and cope with his own boredom might

seem like such a small thing—but it's actually a pretty important moment. And who knows what cool stuff might unfold for a kid left alone with his boredom? Your kid may hit upon a new interest, consider a new insight, or find a new inspiration—you don't want to get in the way of that. Or he may just decide to get off his ass and organize the garage, which would be pretty awesome, too.

YOUR KID TALKS LIKE A SAILOR

◆ ◆ ◆ ◆ ◆ ◆ ◆ ◆

Okay, I realize I sound old and cranky, but I have to begin with this: When I was a kid, "crap" and "piss" and the like were considered bad words. When my fifth grade classmate Tracey passed some gas during math (which she did quite a bit, poor thing), whispering, "She *farted*!" to one another was an illicit thrill, a bad-kid moment that we absolutely reveled in throughout the morning. Only the real troublemakers would say "shit," and "fuck" did not even register as a word we might possibly utter.

Flash forward to today, where our little darlings are matter-of-factly asking, "Who farted?" (at the dinner table, even, OMG), describing themselves as "pissed off" by some setback, and asking what's "all that crap" on their bed (the same crap you've left strewn all over the house this past week, by the way). Once forbidden—or at least highly discouraged, and uttered in thrilled whispers—these words have wormed their way into the everyday vocabulary of just about every kid I know, and almost certainly your own.

Now this may not immediately seem like some huge crisis—but before long you will realize that this profanity is not an end unto itself but actually a gateway to more unpleasant and objectionable language. Among your kid's many appealing jobs as a tween, after all, are pushing the envelope and testing the limits, including the boundaries of acceptable speech—and if "fart" and its ilk have become dinner table words, well, they certainly won't fit the bill. Calling someone an ass or exclaiming, "What the hell!" isn't going to do the trick, either. Your kid needs more. He needs to add "shit" and "fuck" to his vocabulary, and to explore all their charming permutations—you know, "motherfucker," "who the fuck," "shitty," and my personal favorite, "What the fuck? [pause, followed by prolonged, annoyed exhalation] Shit." And if he has his way, your kid will soon be talking like this pretty much all the time—and sounding more like a recently paroled mobster or aspiring rapper than the precious little bunny you know him to be.

So what do you do when you hear "shit," "fuck," and similar issuing from the same mouth that was not all that long ago proudly mastering "mama" and "ball"? Well, it depends. If your kid is with a friend who's dropping a similar number of *s*- and *f*-bombs, you should probably do nothing. I know it's painful, and I know it's probably the influence of the other kid, who you've never really liked and whose parents seemed weird that time you met them, but really, all you can do is sit tight. They're not doing it to bug you, and your kid has probably forgotten you're even there (or is pretending you aren't, even if you're the one driving the car). It's not exactly the time for a parenting intervention, you know? When you and your kid are alone, you can address the issue very briefly with a remark like, "I heard the way you and Seth were talking. I know a lot of kids your age use words like that and that it probably doesn't seem like a big deal. But those words can be offensive, and you should be careful not to use them when adults are around." Even if your kid doesn't react, he will definitely hear you—and when he gets older and less worried about fitting in with his peers, he'll appreciate not only the message but also the way it was delivered.

But what if you are on the receiving end of these utterances? What if someone you know to be at least a somewhat decent person—a teacher or a coach or the kid who up to a second ago you thought was a close friend—is the antecedent of the snarled "motherfucker" or if the dinner you have just prepared or the parenting choice you have just made is being described as "shitty"? Well, then, you have to engage—and engage correctly. It's tempting to laugh it off—you'll avoid a confrontation as well as take the power away from your kid by acting amused rather than angry—but don't. If your kid is merely looking for a reaction, you're teaching him that he's got to go further to get it; and if he's using bad language to unleash frustration or anger he's having trouble expressing otherwise, you're shutting down what could ultimately be a pretty important moment.

When your kid curses like that, react calmly but firmly. Look him in the eye and tell him, "Don't use language like that around me. It's disrespectful to talk to me that way, and you may not do it." This is an important boundary to set; you can't control what kind of language he uses when you're not around, and it may be that he feels compelled to speak that way around his peers in order to maintain his social standing—sad, but true, and you've got to respect it. But don't let that be your last word; leave the door open by adding,

"A lot of times, adults speak that way when they're upset or angry. If there's something you want to talk about, I hope you'll let me know." Unless you can tell by your kid's face that a revelation is imminent, there's no need to say anything further at that point; you've asserted the rules without shaming him or even raising your voice, and that alone is worth celebrating. (So feel free to pause your reading while you pour yourself some champagne or treat yourself to a mani-pedi. I'll wait.)

While you don't want to encourage cursing, it's also not completely fair to act as if letting a "fuck" slip out now and then is like the worst crime ever. After all, your kid is just learning what you and I already know to be true: Cursing is fun! It's empowering when you feel out of control, comforting when you're hurt or angry, totally entertaining to slip into a parenting book about bratty kids—and also pretty useful in dealing with the occasional suckiness of life. Studies have demonstrated, in fact, that cursing can actually help people manage anger and may even reduce physical pain. So develop some substitutes that your entire family can use in place of the actual *s*- and *f*-words; you will be surprised at how effective this can be in expressing negative emotions as well as bringing the family closer. When you or your kid lets fly a "shirt!" or "huck!"—favorites in our home, although I do recommend you be a bit more on the ball than we were and not allow "huck" to morph into "motherhucker," which is not technically profanity but still kind of disturbing—you'll enjoy almost the same stress release that real cursing provides, and you'll also feel bonded, like you share a private code.

One last thought on acceptable language; this the most important of all. While it's easy to get fixated on words like "shit" or "fuck," the words that should be of much more concern are "bitch," "fag," "gay," "pussy," and their equally repulsive cohort. For sure you've heard a kid calling a girl a "bitch," demeaning a boy by calling him a "fag," using "gay" in a negative way, or uttering the word "pussy" in a context other than referring to a small cat. If your kid does this, do not overlook it and tell yourself that this is just how tweens and adolescents talk. You are right, but only partially: This is just how tweens and adolescents talk when they learn from the most hateful elements of popular culture how to treat other people, and it's how tweens and adolescents talk when their parents are too overwhelmed, apathetic, or intimidated to keep their offspring from dabbling in becoming disgusting human beings. This is not how you want your kid to talk, and not who you want your kid to be—so you must tell him firmly, backing up your words with clear explanations ("Calling a girl a bitch doesn't condemn her actions or behavior—it condemns her for being a girl; you may think you're insulting just one person when you say 'bitch,' but that word is actually an insult to every woman you know, including your mom and your grandmothers") and whatever consequences are necessary to drive home the message. And while tweens usually learn this type of language from popular music, the media, or (gross) friends, it's a sad truth that words like "bitch" and "fag" get tossed around in far too many families as well. Whether it's your kid or an adult who should know oh-so-much better talking this way, please do him—and everyone else—a favor by making him shut the huck up.

YOUR KID DRESSES LIKE A PROSTITUTE

◆ ◆ ◆ ◆ ◆ ◆ ◆ ◆

My amazing friend Joelle recently had the following experience with her kid:

Her tween daughter Molly has, over the past few months, shed her glasses, upgraded her wardrobe, and added some makeup to her heretofore natural-girl look. Nothing major, nothing drastic, and nothing that appeared to be interfering with her general sensibleness and wonderfulness. Joelle was, in fact, ready to breathe a big sigh of relief.

Until Molly came home from a weekend at a friend's with a pair of four-inch spike stiletto sandals—sandals that had obviously been stolen from some small-footed hooker but which Molly insisted were the height of sexiness and coolness and something that she intended to wear immediately and often.

Here is what Joelle did not do:

Acquiesce despite her better judgment, because you've got to pick your battles, and Molly's just expressing herself, and Molly will probably wear her down eventually, anyway

Beam as Molly modeled the shoes, telling herself that Molly's youth and beauty must surely reflect on her and resolving to relive her own glory days through her adolescent daughter

Scream at Molly for even thinking of wearing such a thing, and remind Molly furiously that she is not raising her daughter to be a disgusting slut

Here's what Joelle did:

One, she took a deep breath—always a good thing, particularly when the image of Molly even touching these shoes was causing palpitations. Next, she pasted a nonchalant smile on her face and told her daughter, "Great, put them on. I'll drop you off at the North Trail"—an area of town famous for its streetwalkers and by-the-hour motels—"and you can earn a few bucks while I make dinner."

There was, Joelle admitted, a tense moment. I can totally picture Molly looking at her mom, sizing up the situation, deciding what the next move should be. But Joelle had built a foundation of mutual respect with her daughter, kept open the lines of communication, taught Molly to question rather than blindly accept society's views on what makes a woman attractive. So the moment passed; Molly burst out laughing, and that was the end of the shoes.

Let me be super clear: I do not think Joelle was genuinely prepared to shuttle her daughter off for a night (well, an evening—Molly does have a curfew) of turning tricks, nor am I suggesting you consider prostitution as a career choice for your own kid, even though she may have exactly the right wardrobe. I am not even sharing this story because I think it will work for you. (In fact, it was such a great and unique moment that it may not work for anyone again, ever.) I share it because, well, it's just so awesome—but also because it demonstrates a really important aspect of your campaign to get your kid to put on some decent clothes, or at least some shorts that actually cover her ass.

Here's the deal: This campaign can't begin the day your daughter comes downstairs drenched in scented body glitter, sporting a microskirt and thong, and pronouncing herself ready for a trip to the mall with friends. It must begin many years earlier, when she receives her first training manual for an adolescence where her self-worth is determined by how she looks and how pleasing she is to men.

You don't remember that manual in the pile of books you devotedly read to your daughter every night, in the long-ago era when she'd snuggle up to you and actually ask to hear the sound of your voice? It's a sneaky one; its messages are hidden in classic princess stories (where the triumphant heroines are beautiful and the mean stepsisters are ugly, and where the little mermaid snags her guy by remaining completely silent), onesies proclaiming a baby girl "Mommy's Little Shopper" ("Mommy's Little Astrophysicist" having failed to catch on), and television shows and movies where boys control most of the action or where girls take center stage but engage primarily in activities like planning a tea party or corralling their ill-behaved-but-clearly-having-the-better-time little brother (I'm talking to you, *Max & Ruby*!). The manual also teaches your daughter to notice how often she's praised for being pretty, cute, and sweet rather than adventurous, bold, and funny—and to realize that her tantrums and moments of rudeness will go unpunished as long as they're characterized as the outbursts of a diva or a drama queen.

So yeah, your kid probably knows the manual quite well. And that's just what the fashion designers are counting on when your daughter grows old enough to choose her own clothes—that she'll gravitate toward the items that conform to the gender expectations she's been taught. They're counting on her to choose the teeny bikini over a swimsuit she won't have to rearrange every time she jumps into the water, to think sweatpants bearing suggestive messages are sassy and fun, and to don uncomfortable kitten heels for everyday wear because "even though I can't really move around in them," a fourth grader explained earnestly, "they're totally cute."

In short, much of the world is arrayed against your kid—so you need to be ready as well. But *how*?

Ironically, one of the best ways to hooker-proof your kid is not to focus on the hooker-wear—at least not right away. Your tween is at an age where—despite the way she sometimes acts—she is interested in your opinion and cares what you think; even if she doesn't appear to be listening, she's definitely filing the messages you send and the values you espouse. She also wants to share her life with you—not necessarily the details of her crush, but the songs she likes, the celebrities she admires, the videos she watches. So let her do it! Ask questions, let her tell you how a particular song makes her feel or what she finds appealing about a particular celebrity, and tell her—in a matter-of-fact, nonjudgmental way—what you think as well. "I agree that song is exciting to listen to. I feel uncomfortable with some of the lyrics, though—I think they sound disrespectful of women and girls. What do you think?" "Yes, she is supertalented. She really has a unique style, too—do you like it?" "That's an amazing video. I noticed that the guys in the video were wearing regular clothes, but the women were wearing really sexy clothes. What do you think about that?" Glimpsing this part of her world and engaging in conversation about it will give you an essential sense of who your kid is and who she's becoming—and will also give you a chance to wield some influence.

But what if it's too late? What if she's already clamoring for clothes you consider wildly inappropriate or already has a closet stuffed with things-you-hate-to-let-her-out-of-the-house-in-but-all-her-friends-are-wearing? Then your first job is to be the parent everyone seems to resent but always respects, at least later in life, and say no. It's not hard once you get used to it—you just need to be firm in your belief that you're doing the right thing and convey a sense of authority and finality: "I know you want to wear that, but the answer is no." Offer a brief, concise explanation, but don't get dragged into a big debate: "A skirt that short/a dress that tight/shorts that small don't show respect for your body, and they're not allowed." "I hear that Olivia has that exact outfit, but that doesn't make it okay. Those clothes aren't appropriate for anyone your age."

Yes, she'll seethe, because she's a tween and it's part of her job. But another part of her job is being mercurial, so she'll switch moods soon enough—and when she does, you can deepen your "no" by exploring the implications of the clothing she wants and invite her to share her feelings about what it means to be attractive: "What do you like about clothes like this? Why do you think so many girls your age want to wear that? Why do you think parents might not want their kids to dress that way? Why do you think stores don't make clothes like this for boys?" You can even introduce her to the training manual she's been absorbing for so many years by flipping through a magazine or online ads together; note how women in bikinis are used to sell beer, how dangerously thin women are airbrushed to look, or how hollow-eyed and miserable the models in bridal magazines appear (this was pointed out to me by my then eight-year-old daughter, and it's actually kind of hilarious)—and talk about how these images can lead women to feel their looks are the most important thing they have to offer, and to develop unrealistic expectations of how they should dress and behave.

Will this lesson induce your kid to cover up? Maybe not right away, in which case repeat the paragraph on saying no as needed. But it will give her a new perspective from which to regard microskirts and short shorts and sweats proclaiming her butt "Sexy" and "Fabulous"—and in this world of parenting tweens, that is definitely a most excellent start.

YOUR KID DOES REALLY STUPID STUFF

◆ ◆ ◆ ◆ ◆ ◆ ◆ ◆

Did you know that when you think your family is having a slow, lazy day, and you are lolling around reading *Us*, musing how lucky you are that your kids have reached the age where they can entertain themselves and do not require your vigilant attention at every moment—well, this is not actually the time to relax said vigilant attention? At least not if you are living with my tween son, because he will choose exactly that moment to stroll by with the casual announcement that he is going to do a science experiment in the front yard.

"Sounds great," I murmured, eyes still glued to "Who Wore It Best?" as I silently congratulated myself on raising such a curious and intellectual kid. Then some survival instinct kicked in, and I looked up to realize that clutched in my kid's hands was not a magnifying glass nor a bottle of vinegar and a box of baking soda nor even some Diet Coke and Mentos (which is awesome, try it)—but a large container of Purell and a book of matches.

The fact that I am writing this at my breakfast table rather than from the smoldering ruins of my home will indicate that I got off my ass and managed this particular situation, a course of action I urge if your kid is inclined to pursue a similar hands-on study of flammable liquids. However, if the same kid breezes by your station on the couch a few weeks later holding a box of orange Rit dye, a bunch of T-shirts, and your old roasting pan, may I recommend you stop yourself from jumping up, demanding to know what in the world he is up to this time, and appointing yourself his official supervisor? Because while the possibility of a large brush fire breaking out in your ground cover requires some significant and immediate parental attention, the prospect of your kid's blundering his first attempt at tie-dyeing some old clothes is a great occasion to stand down and let him do his thing.

I understand: Your kid is so excited to tie-dye—but you know he doesn't really know what he's doing and he's going to end up not only ruining his shirts but feeling let down and disappointed to boot. There's also the matter of your driveway—though your kid has assured you that the guy on his favorite YouTube channel has assured him that Rit does not stain cement, you have your suspicions. And finally, isn't this a teachable moment for your kid—a chance for you to show him that he needs to consider these little adventures more carefully, that he can't dive into projects so haphazardly, that attention to detail and meticulous planning are the keys to success?

Well, yes and no. That is, yes, your worries are all legitimate: In the initial encounter between your tween and some new challenge—tie-dye, a research paper, a thousand-piece building project, a leadership role at school, breaking into a new group of friends, taking up an unfamiliar sport—the loser is likely to be your kid. He will screw up the dye job, forget to use the proper heading, misplace piece number 743, disappoint his peers or himself, throw an air ball as the game clock buzzes. But no: None of that means that you get to follow your kid around, spouting unsolicited advice and commenting on all the things he should be doing differently, evaluating and guiding and correcting—even and maybe especially if you know better.

Here's the thing: Your kid is a tween, and being a tween means making the transition from child to young adult, from needful dependence to confident autonomy. This path is not, shall we say, the smoothest of roads; it's a tough one, and your kid will confront plenty of setbacks along the way—many of his own making. But as much as you'll want to parachute in and help him (maybe even carry him) over every rough spot, you just can't. Being the parent of a tween means letting your kid learn and grow and mature, and sometimes he'll need to do that the hard way—by doing really stupid stuff, and experiencing the consequences.

Now I'm not advocating an entirely hands-free approach to your kid's tween years, especially after that close encounter with my own kid and the bottle of Purell. And if the stupid stuff your kid is doing entails an immediate threat to himself, someone else, or your property, yeah, that's a good time to get involved. But if you take a deep breath and consider the situation before you jump in, you will probably find that that's rarely the case. What's far more likely is that your kid's doing something that will bring disagreeable consequences: embarrassment, frustration, a foot dyed orange, or a bad grade on a school project. And while of course you'd prefer that your precious sweetheart not suffer such unpleasantness, it's really the only way for him to develop resourcefulness and resilience, to bounce back from disappointment and failure—and to complete his journey to independence and adulthood.

Because while it would be awesome if we could grow up without making mistakes, looking like idiots, regretting actions, and failing now and then—that's not actually the way the world works. And it's a good thing for your kid to experience these less-than-wonderful aspects of life while he's young enough to shake them off and learn from them: A fifth grader getting a C minus and "I'm disappointed!" scrawled in red across an essay he wrote during breakfast the day it was due may be upset and embarrassed, for example, but he's a lot better off than an eighteen-year-old shattered by her failure to totally ace an Achievement Test she took the morning after a Bangles concert (wait, that was me); and a twelve-year-old who ignores your instructions to reapply sunscreen throughout the day on his class's end-of-the-year trip to a water park may end up pretty uncomfortable, but he'll definitely be more meticulous the next hundred times he goes in the sun. Really, it's an incontrovertible truth that your kid is going to mess up somewhere between here and, say, his fortieth birthday; and once you accept that fact, you'll find it much easier to let him make those mistakes now—while he's under your roof, under your influence, and under the age where the consequences of thoughtlessness or poor planning or just plain stupidity could truly imperil his future.

In the short term, watching your kid like a hawk and guiding him away from every possible bad choice might seem appealing:

You'll ensure your kid's success, demonstrate your never-ending care, and impart to him the right way of doing things—and isn't that what being a good parent is all about? Well, uh, no. This strategy loses its luster pretty quickly: You'll become so enmeshed with your kid that you'll lose sight of where his success begins and yours ends, you'll annoy and alienate him with your never-ending care, and you'll deprive him of the opportunity to learn the right way of doing things—at least, the right way for him.

Renegotiating your strategy may require you not only to renegotiate the way you interact with your tween but also to renegotiate the boundaries between the two of you. And if your reaction to this statement is incredulous distaste and/or a haughty, self-righteous rejoinder that there are no boundaries between you and your tween—he's the most important thing in your life, and you are right by his side in everything he does—well, I'm actually talking especially to you.

Why you? Because your kid needs some space to do all the learning and growing and maturing it's time for him to do, and he won't get it unless you, to put it directly, back off. Of course it's totally awesome to be involved in your kid's life, to support his efforts and interests, to celebrate his ups and commiserate with his downs—but it's not fair to you or to your kid to have this be the entire focus of your own existence. Your kid deserves to explore and try and bungle and recover without worrying how his every action will reflect on you, his hovering parent; and you deserve to watch your kid's life unfold without suffering an anxiety attack every time he does something dumb.

Another bonus of letting your kid do something stupid every now and then? It will, in the long term, anyway, make your life much easier. When college applications loom, and your kid is expected to manufacture an essay about overcoming hardships or demonstrating grit or learning from misfortune, he will not look at you with the bewilderment and confusion that can arise only in a kid not once allowed to fall on his ass, let alone forced to pick himself up and try again; and you will not feel obligated to trundle this kid who's never made a mistake off for a summer of digging wells in South America or mooching off a host family in rural India. Simply by allowing your kid's life to progress according to the choices he makes—the good and the bad, the smart and the stupid—you will provide him with plenty of fodder for an amazing essay. You will also inoculate your future self against frantic phone calls and desperate texts from your future kid, a coddled tween now all grown up and helplessly flailing around the ocean we call adulthood, woefully unprepared to navigate the challenges of real life—and with absolutely no clue how to tie-dye a shirt to boot.

YOUR KID RULES OVER YOU

◆ ◆ ◆ ◆ ◆ ◆ ◆ ◆

Transcript of a recent conversation with my nine-year-old son:

SON: Mom, can I have Panera for lunch one day? (Panera being one of those bakery-café chains with oversized muffins and rather excellent soup-in-a-bread-bowl.)

ME (already getting excited for soup): Sure, we can go to Panera one day! Maybe I'll take you this weekend.

SON (after awkward pause): Actually, I meant maybe you could bring me Panera for lunch. Like, at school.

ME: Like, I would go to Panera in the middle of the day, pick up lunch, and we would eat it in the cafeteria?

SON (after another awkward pause and some crinkling of the face, apparently concerned that this exchange is not proceeding as he hoped): Well, not we. You would get it for me and, you know, drop it off.

ME (confusion giving way to understanding and complete annoyance): So I would basically arrange my day around making a trip to Panera to buy you lunch, then I would take it to you at school and just leave? Why on earth would I do a thing like that?

SON (wearing expression of utter defeat): I don't know. Ryan's mom does it every day.

After further questioning, I learned that young Ryan does not care for the lunches served at school, nor does he enjoy the PB&J-in-an-insulated-bag option. In these preferences Ryan is like pretty much every kid I have ever known, including myself; to this day a fish stick gives me flashbacks to the fourth grade hot lunch where—well, I digress. Obvious responses to Ryan's dilemma might include advising him to pack his own sack lunch featuring food he actually likes, or the formerly popular admonition to Suck It Up. But Ryan's mother has hit upon another solution, one being replicated in schools and homes and other gathering places for children throughout this fair land: Completely surrender yourself in order to spare your kid a modicum of unpleasantness.

Why does Ryan merit daily delivery service of his favorite lunch? For the same reason twelve-year-old Mason relaxes at the table while his mother prepares his scrambled egg whites and soy breakfast sausage, Bronwyn's parents frantically begin assembling care packages weeks before she leaves for camp, and hundreds of highly educated adults spend every single Saturday procuring healthful snacks for pint-sized soccer players and manning Girl Scout cookie–selling booths rather than kicking back with a beer or getting a pedicure. Because we have taken our (entirely understandable and commendable) love for our children to truly insane heights of devotion, perhaps forgetting in the process that we have the right to be grown-ups with grown-up needs and grown-up lives, and instead falling prey to the terrible illusion that being a good parent means being our kid's constant cheerleader, chauffeur, and all-around concierge.

Now, I am not suggesting you tell your kid she can't become a Girl Scout because you'd rather hang out sipping chocolate martinis than help her acquire an Animal Habitats badge (even though it's true, I mean, yuck) or deny your offspring the opportunity to participate in team sports or refuse to cook her waffles on lazy weekend mornings. But I am suggesting that you have a teeny voice inside that lets you know when you're going too far for your kid—a teeny voice that causes your chest to constrict or your blood pressure to rise or a flash of annoyance to interrupt your stream of devoted ministrations when one too many demands is being made—and that you listen to that voice instead of ordering it to shut up for fear it will turn you into a Neglectful Parent.

Because it won't. That teeny voice is actually your best friend. It will assure you that your kid will not break if you answer the plaintive announcement that she's hungry with the matter-of-fact suggestion that she make herself a sandwich (putting the bread away afterward would be a nice touch), if you inform her that she will have to miss Lily's spa party because you have other plans, or if you show up at camp visiting day bearing smiles, hugs, and a couple of treats rather than staggering under the weight of bags of food more appropriate to the liberation of POWs. That teeny voice is reminding you that although your kid is superimportant—and yes, I understand, she is really, really superimportant—she is still not the actual center of the universe and that it is okay for her to realize that you have interests besides shuttling her to tap and hand-washing her tights and fulfilling her every demand. And that teeny voice will comfort you that rather than descending into the realm of Neglectful Parent, you are actually lifting your kid up from the valley of Insufferable Brats.

Really, people! Remember how you faced down those mean girls in seventh grade? Remember making it through your driver's test and snagging your first job and surviving your sorority formal date's throwing up on your shoes during "Wonderful Tonight"? You are strong! So you should not be afraid to tell your third grader, "I know you want to join the travel team, but the schedule means we won't be able to spend weekends as a family all season, and that won't work for us." Just listen to that teeny voice and do it. Let her express her dismay, and help her try to find an alternative—a less demanding team, a more manageable sport—but don't apologize for putting your extremely legitimate adult needs and the welfare of the family over her nine-year-old desires. When your kid wants to go roller-skating for the second Saturday in a row, and you still have the headache from last week's outing, don't plaster on a smile and chirp, "What a fun idea!"—simply tell her you're not up for that again. And when she delivers a request from her fifth grade teacher that you type up her classmates' handwritten essays so they will look more presentable when displayed on Student Project Night, laugh derisively and say, "You guys are old enough to type your own stuff. Anyway, that will cut into my leisure time." (Do suggest, however, that your child be more discreet than mine and not repeat this response verbatim to her teacher.)

Despite your discomfort with declining any opportunity to demonstrate your unending devotion, your kid will in fact benefit from adapting to a supporting rather than a starring role in life. She will come to understand that the entire family unit must be honored and that parents are fully formed human beings with needs and wants at least as important as her own. And while she is honing these genuinely essential insights, you, my friend, can sip away on your chocolate martini—and help me cyberstalk the asshole who threw up on my shoes.

ACKNOWLEDGMENTS

I offer endless and abundant thanks to all of the wonderful people who helped bring *Your Kid's a Brat and It's All Your Fault* into being. Infinite gratitude to my incredible agents Caitlen Rubino-Bradway, who not only knows how to craft a book proposal and sell a manuscript like no other but who also introduced me to the croissants at Le Pain Quotidien, and Lauren Galit; to my fabulous editor Sara Carder, whose enthusiasm for this book meant the world to me; to Lori Lesser, who is not only my favorite attorney but also one of my favorite people in general; and to the entire team at TarcherPerigee, especially Joanna Ng, Keely Platte, and Brittany Saghi. I am so happy to have worked with all of you.

Thank you, thank you, thank you to my friends who believed in this project, who graciously allowed me to share their joyful, triumphant, and occasionally less-than-glorious parenting moments, and who know that I am actually a lot nicer than I sound in this book. (Seriously, if you met me in person, you would really like me.)

Extra special appreciation to Sharon Kunkel, Faith and Jason Lipton, Sara Malone, Amy Nance, Michele Reich, Daniel Shuchman, Alicia Paul Zoller, and especially and always Laurie Buchsbaum, who understands everything. I love you guys.

Speaking of love, thanks above all to my amazing husband and children. You are the best things in the world.

Elaine Rose Glickman

APPENDIX A

HELPFUL PHRASES TO USE WITH YOUR KID

Remember how totally tongue-tied you got every time your middle school crush came around? For whatever unsettling reason, the sensation's not all that different from the what-do-I-say-and-how-do-I-handle-this feeling that arises when your kid does something especially, er, challenging. Here you'll find thirty quick, useful phrases that will help you respond to common problems or defuse tough situations; some you'll recognize from previous chapters, and some are brand spanking new. Commit them to memory and pull them out as needed.

FOR YOUR YOUNGER KID

"I hear you want to sit in the chair, but I'm sitting here. You can sit on my lap or on the couch."

"I'll be ready to listen as soon as you're ready to use your nice voice."

"You do not hurt me. It's okay to be angry, but it is never okay to hurt me."

"You are safe when I'm gone, and I will always come back."

"I can see you don't like what's on your plate, but this is what we have to eat."

"I know it's hard to take turns, but sharing is the right thing to do."

"Is your piece of cake too big or just right?"

"Do you want to leave the playground now or in five minutes?"

"Would you like help putting on your socks, yes, please, or no, thank you?"

"It's someone else's turn to talk."

"As soon as you finish cleaning up your toys, we can watch *Frozen.*"

"No."

FOR YOUR OLDER KID

"Sometimes people lie because they don't want to get into trouble, but lying is worse than getting into trouble."

"That is disrespectful, and you may not speak to me that way."

"That sounds great, but we can't afford it."

"I support the things that are important to you, and I expect you to do the same."

"I trust you to handle that yourself."

"This is my decision to make."

"I hear you're mad/sad/frustrated/upset, and I'd love to talk about it when you're ready."

"I know you want to wear that, but the answer is no."

"I love you too much to let you behave this way."

"I'm all done talking about this."

"Because I said so."

"No."

AND A FEW BONUS PHRASES TO HELP FOSTER POSITIVE INTERACTIONS AND HAPPY TIMES

"Let's read a book/go to the park/watch a movie/play a game/grab coffee together."

"I'm so glad to see you!"

"What do you think? I'd really like to hear your opinion."

"Can you teach me how to do that?"

"I know we clash sometimes, but honestly, I could not ask for a better son/daughter."

"I love you."

APPENDIX B

HELPFUL TASKS TO GIVE YOUR KID

You know your tween ought to get off her ass and help out around the house—but what exactly should she do? And what's this rumor you've heard about school-age kids—and even preschoolers—being capable of useful and honest labor? The fabulous truth is that kids of every age and stage can do something to contribute to the household—and, in fact, they should. Carrying out helpful tasks and taking responsibility for regular chores instills all sorts of positive values in your kid—a strong work ethic, a sense of cooperation, an appreciation for physical labor, an understanding of what it takes to manage a household, an affinity for the vacuum cleaner, an immunity to the disgustingness of cat puke (read on for proof!)—and also gives you some time to put your feet up and contemplate even more ways for your kid to build character while getting shit done. It's win-win, I'm telling you.

Your kid may surprise you by jumping eagerly into this new

lifestyle—but then again, she may not. She will probably prove more cooperative, however, if you take the advice of some of my amazing friends, whose kids are not only smart, funny, and delightful but have also become competent launderers, accomplished cooks, and not-always-grim draggers of large garbage cans up a huge hill on trash day:

Start them young. My friend Stacie has a motto in her house: "You make the mess, you clean the mess." While it may be tough to establish this as the family creed once your kid hits her tweens, Stacie started it while her kid was still a toddler—and at four, he not only cleans up his toys but even puts away his own clothes. Did I mention he's four?

Don't say "chores." My friend Andrea talks to her kid about being "a good citizen of the house," and my friend Amy W. calls chores "expectations." You may think it's all semantics, but Andrea's ten-year-old washes his own school uniform, and Amy's kid was cooking pretty good meals as soon as she could see over the stove-top, so I would listen to them if I were you.

Let consequences unfold. Get your kid to help out by letting her feel the consequences of not helping out. For example: My friend Jason's kid is responsible for doing her own laundry—so if she doesn't have anything clean to wear, she's the one frantically running a load of wash. My friend Amy S.'s kid strips and helps make up his bed with fresh sheets—so if he balks at doing his part, he may not have the most comfortable sleep in the world.

Ready to hear some specifics and get started? Just consult the handy list below—quick, before your kid destroys it! And yes, every entry reflects an actual job performed by an actual kid in her actual home—no actors or hired hands allowed—and no, no kid was harmed in the making of this appendix.

"Jobs for Toddlers"

Your young kid can develop gross and fine motor skills, practice math, get some exercise, and learn empathy and responsibility, all while staying (mostly) out of your hair and even making himself useful! Best of all, he'll cherish the opportunity to help out and to be an active partner in whatever his grown-ups are doing. Enjoy the (sadly brief) association between chores and fun, and keep your toddler or preschooler busy and engaged with these helpful tasks:

Clearing his dishes (this will go much better if you use unbreakable dishes, by the way)

Sorting laundry (making piles of whites and colors is inexplicably absorbing to many a young kid—just go with it)

Bringing in groceries (though you may want to carry the omega-3 eggs yourself)

Watering plants (with supervision, at least until your kid apprehends the difference between watering plants and drowning them, or watering plants and watering himself)

Light dusting (a bright orange feather duster was my favorite toy when I was small—yes, I was a weird kid, but my mom was clearly a genius)

Feeding a pet (again with supervision lest the pet go from feast to famine depending on your kid's mood)

Turning off lights (this will foster environmental awareness in your kid, satisfy his desire to boss you around, and save money to boot; even if he's too small to reach the light switch, he's definitely not too small to remind you—loudly—that you've left a light on)

Serving as a "runner" (taking old papers from your desk to the recycling bin—this presupposes that you actually follow through on your long-laid plan to clean out said desk—or ferrying expired tubs of yogurt and the leftover kale salad you never got around to eating to the garbage can—assuming that you get around to cleaning the fridge, too)

Putting away toys (of course!—have I taught you nothing so far?)

"Child Labor"

Your school-age kid is ready to take on more responsibility—and the more you give her, the better for you both. The skills she'll acquire, the sense of duty she'll cultivate, and the trustworthiness and reliability she'll develop are exactly what you want in your rapidly maturing kid—plus, your house will look awesome (well, awesomer). It's also a lot easier to instill the habit of helpfulness now than when your kid is a tween—so don't delay.

Sweeping and light vacuuming (remember how the broom and vacuum cleaner fascinated your kid when she was small?—lucky her, she's finally old enough to use them!)

Setting and clearing the table (it will take some effort to establish this routine, especially if you insist your kid do a better-than-slipshod job—but it will give you a helper at mealtime, which is great)

Loading and unloading the dishwasher (aren't you so over being the anonymous fairy who magically transforms dirty dishes into clean, and even makes them appear in their proper places in the cabinet?—it's time to pass the torch, er, wand)

Putting away laundry (this is a fantastic one—and you can gradually increase your kid's laundry-related responsibilities so she's ready to do it all when she hits the tween years)

Emptying the trash cans and recycling bins (this won't take nearly as long if your kid stops complaining and just does it, plus she may find some interesting stuff if she pokes around—seriously, be careful what you throw away!)

Wiping down countertops and mirrors (your kid might actually have fun using a spray bottle and rag, not to mention seeing the instant results her efforts bring)

Cleaning up common areas (if your kid does a good job organizing and clearing the clutter, let her do a little rearranging of your framed photos and display pieces—she'll be flattered and probably really enjoy it)

Cleaning out the car (especially when your kid whines about what a mess your car is—it's probably mostly her shit, anyway; teach her how to wash the outside as well—you consider it an annoying chore, but she may consider it an awesome treat)

Preparing the marketing list (give your kid a glimpse behind the scenes of your, ahem, smoothly running home by having her keep track of which staples are running low and what groceries are needed)

"Tasks for Tweens"

Your kid may beg to differ, but a tween is actually capable of just about every household job there is. And the more useful tasks your kid undertakes, the more engaged he'll be. Think of chores not as drudgery or punishment, but as fantastic opportunities for your growing kid to contribute to the household—and think of your kid not as a cranky workhorse but as a potential partner in upholding and caring for the home you share. Yes, I'm serious.

Preparing meals (don't stop once your kid has mastered the arts of making sandwiches, chopping vegetables, and scrambling eggs—with a little guidance and encouragement, he can totally get dinner on the table)

Caring for a pet (feeding, watering, and walking are great—but your kid can also be changing the kitty litter, picking up poops, and even cleaning up cat vomit; I just learned that my friend Sharon's kid does this—my kid starts tomorrow, and yours should, too)

Deeper cleaning (regular vacuuming, scrubbing shelves in the pantry and fridge, washing floors, and even cleaning the bathrooms are tween-appropriate tasks)

Taking out the garbage and recycling (this weekly trash-day haul was made for tweens, in my opinion)

Gardening and weeding (this can actually be fun on a cool or overcast day—plus, your kid will get some fresh air and feel more invested in your garden, landscaping, and home in general)

Checking your tires (teach your kid to use a tire gauge, and let him have at it—he'll help you out as well as learn the basics of maintaining the Lamborghini Reventón he plans to own someday)

Heavy lifting (carrying hefty grocery bags, schlepping big suitcases, and filling the water softener with huge bags of salt—if your kid is big and strong enough to handle it, let him)

Dealing with the mail (from sorting bills and recycling junk mail to—under supervision!—setting up autopay accounts and renewing magazine subscriptions; this is a great way for your kid to practice life skills while pitching in)

Sending gifts (you may not have the time or inclination to peruse a gallery of online greetings in order to find the perfect e-card for Aunt Evelyn's birthday or feel able to choose between a bouquet of flowers or fruit for your parents' anniversary—but your kid almost certainly will; let your kid fill the online cart—just be sure you are the sole keeper of the PayPal password)

One final note: The most important thing about giving your kid helpful tasks is ensuring that he contributes appropriately to the household—he should feel like a valued member of the team, not a beneficiary of your (endless) unpaid labor. But not every job is right for every kid, so depending on your kid's temperament and strengths, feel free to add to—or take away from—this list. Just don't dismiss the "cleaning up cat vomit" option too quickly, okay? I mean, that is classic.

APPENDIX C

REAL-LIFE Q&A ABOUT OTHER PEOPLE'S KIDS

If you haven't had enough of me bossing people around, check out this real-life Q&A from my parenting advice column. The letters might help you, guide you, inspire you—or just comfort you to know that somebody out there has it a hell of a lot worse than you.

"Should I Stop Changing in Front of My Kid?"

What is the age my kids should be when I start closing the bathroom door fully or not changing clothes in front of them? I find that I have started to turn around if they are in the room when I am changing. I don't want to draw attention to this, but I'm not sure why or how to explain it. What type or how much partial nudity, in your opinion, is appropriate for children of various ages to see of their parents?

If you have started to turn around when you are changing, your children are probably too old to see you without your clothes on, and it's probably time to start closing the bathroom door as well. The "right" age will be different for different families (though it's usually between ages three and five), but your feelings are a good indicator on this one; and your instincts seem to be telling you that it's time to make a change—ack, please pardon the pun.

There's no need to create a big deal over it; make an effort to change when your children are engaged with something else, or hand them a book or your phone and nonchalantly slide the bathroom door shut behind you when nature calls. When they do notice and comment, answer in a matter-of-fact way: "When kids get to be big like you are, it's time for parents to have privacy when they're getting dressed and using the bathroom. If you ever need me when I'm changing or using the bathroom, just knock on the door and tell me what's going on." This explanation will serve as a good introduction to an important issue (it might also lead into a discussion of private parts, if you haven't already broached that subject) while assuring your kids that you remain available and attentive—even if they no longer have front-row seats to the "Mommy Squeezing into Skinny Jeans" revue.

"My Kid Called a Little Boy 'Fat'"

In the supermarket, my four-year-old said, "Mom, look at that big fat kid!" and I could instantly see from the other child's face that he heard my daughter's comment about him. I don't think she was saying it to be mean. How do I explain this to her, and how do I handle the situation?

Imagine for a moment that your child was not the otherwise-adorable four-year-old girl making the comment but instead the overweight boy at whom it was directed. It feels awful, doesn't it? If something like that happens, handle the incident promptly—it gives us the opportunity to do the right thing and provides a teachable moment for our kids. You might tell her gently but firmly, "I know you didn't say that to be mean, but calling people 'fat' hurts their feelings and is not okay. I'm going to tell the little boy we're sorry for hurting his feelings." Then, with your daughter in tow, approach the little boy and say, "Excuse me. I want to apologize for what my little girl said. I'm sure it hurt your feelings, and I'm very sorry." Don't drag the episode out or make your daughter mutter an apology; you don't want to embarrass the boy any further, or your daughter for that matter. With your actions, you will have modeled for her respectful treatment of others, taking responsibility for our actions, and the importance of guarding our words.

Since this episode is long past, you can still share the same general message with your daughter, though it's unlikely to have the same impact. Simply remind her that, although she can tell you anything, the word "fat" can hurt people's feelings and that comments about how other people look should be saved until you two are alone. You might also want to find out what "fat" means to your daughter, and be sure the TV shows she's watching—and the conversations she's overhearing—are teaching her about kindness, respect for others, and a positive body image.

"My Kid Asked to See What Tongue Kissing Looks Like"

Out of the blue one weekend, our six-year-old son asked us what tongue kissing was . . . and if Daddy and I ever did it because he wanted to see what it looked like. My husband gave an impromptu tongue-in-cheek (pun unintended!) demonstration: He bent both of his lips outward to make a big wet fishy mouth and then let his tongue slither all around, Jabba the Hutt style, hugging me and saying in a funny voice, "Lemme give ya a kiss, c'mon, what's wrong, let's tongue kiss." So both kids just cracked up hysterically over that, and then (thankfully) the subject naturally moved on. I guess I'm comfortable with that kind of deflection for now, but what answer do you give when they are a little older—or when they ask a second time?

Hopefully your child will indeed ask a second time, or find a useful book at some point—otherwise, his dates will go home extremely unhappy, not to mention very wet. I totally understand why your husband chose to deflect the question with a Jabba the Hutt imitation—it can be embarrassing to be asked these questions by our children, especially when the questions appear to come out of the blue. However, your child is at a stage where he can be expected to be curious about such matters—and how nice that he felt comfortable coming to you guys with his question, instead of burying it or (eek) attempting to Google "tongue kiss." When these questions come up, answer matter-of-factly with as much appropriate information as you can muster: "When grown-ups tongue kiss, they kiss on the lips and open their mouths so they can touch their tongues together. It probably sounds pretty gross, because you're a kid and it's not something for kids to do." An actual demonstration may be a bit much, and you can tell him that: "Tongue kissing is something most grown-ups do in private, but now you know what it means." And always end these conversations on a positive note: "That was a really good question," or "I know you were curious, and I'm really glad you asked me." These are important lines of communication to open—and keep open!—with our children.

"Can I Take My Kid into the Women's Restroom?"

My son is seven years old, but I'm not entirely comfortable with having him wait outside the door for me when I'm using a public restroom. Is it still okay for me to bring him inside with me? I would worry with him outside the door the whole time, but I also worry that someone is going to come in the women's restroom and chide me for having a boy that is too old to be in there. How do you handle this?

I know seven-year-old boys who can take meticulous care of themselves for far longer than you'd ever want to be in a public bathroom, and seven-year-old boys who will get into some disastrous scrape in the time it takes you to pee and wash your hands—and don't you dare ask, "Well, what if I don't wash my hands?" So it really depends. Chances are great that your son will be perfectly fine if you leave him outside the ladies' room, but taking him inside with you still keeps you within the parameters of "reasonable parent." Assuming your son is not peering over the stalls or making eyes at the other restroom patrons, his accompanying you is really no one else's business, which of course provides no guarantee that someone won't chide you, anyway. Simply ignore any disapproving looks; and if someone does verbally reprimand you, grace her with a gigantic smile and enthusiastic "Thanks for your concern!" While she's trying to figure out how on earth to respond to that one, dry your hands and make your getaway.

"My Kid Asked If I've Ever Tried Drugs"

I know you are supposed to be open about talking to your kids about sex, alcohol, drugs, etc., so we have always encouraged our kids to approach us with any questions they may have. This has worked great until the other day, when my ten-year-old came home from school with questions about a presentation they'd had that day about the dangers of drugs—his question was if my husband or I have ever tried drugs! I was stunned into silence for a second, which I'm worried revealed that my answer was not a definite and absolute no, but I managed to evade answering further. But what do I say if (when?) he asks again? I don't want to lie, but I also don't want to get into the details with my son, or have to explain to a fourth grader that Mommy smoking a little pot during college does not equate to meth addiction or the other scary stuff they spoke about at school.

Good for you for fostering open and honest communication with your son—and for recognizing that some communication may be too open and too honest! You are right that regaling your son with tales of your college days is not the way to go here. He's not seeking the dates and times you may have dabbled in drugs—he's just seeking confirmation that you share the values he's learning at school and that he can look to you as a role model and a guide. And whether you inhaled or not, that is confirmation you can definitely provide. If he brings the topic up again, don't feel obligated to give a direct answer; instead tell him how glad you and your husband are that he's learning to say no to drugs and how important it is that he treat his body with respect and take care of himself. Say that these are really important values in your family and that you can tell he is on the right path. This won't completely distract him from his original question, but it will reinforce the message you want him to receive—and it may satisfy him, particularly if you follow up by commenting that you are totally in the mood for a large dish of ice cream and would he like one as well.

Also from TarcherPerigee:

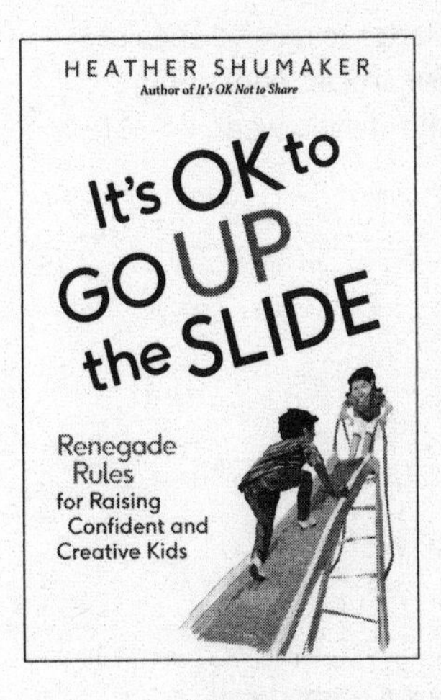

"In her thought-provoking new book, Shumaker challenges some of our assumptions as parents and teachers. She shows us clearly and candidly what kids truly need. This is a helpful and inspiring read for anyone concerned with raising the next generations of healthy children."

—Michael Gurian, author of *The Wonder of Boys* and *The Wonder of Girls*

978-0-399-17200-7

$16.00

"If there's one thing parents need to teach their kids—well beyond getting into college or finding a job—it's how to be humble, contributing citizens of the world. If you're a weary parent trying to do just that, you'll find encouragement and practical know-how in the clear and enjoyable pages of this book."

—Daniel H. Pink, *New York Times* bestselling author of *Drive: The Surprising Truth About What Motivates Us*

978-0-399-16997-7

$26.95